STECK-VAUGHN

Building Strategies
for GED Success

Social Studies

Steck
Vaughn™

A Harcourt Achieve Imprint

www.Steck-Vaughn.com
1-800-531-5015

STAFF CREDITS

Design: Amy Braden, Deborah Diver, Joyce Spicer
Editorial: Gabrielle Field, Heera Kang, Ellen Northcutt

PHOTOGRAPHY

Page 9 Clay Bennett/©The Christian Science Monitor. All rights reserved; p.11 ©Associated Press/APWideWorld; p.12 ©Northwind Archives; p.13 ©Topham/The Image Works; p.16 ©Northwind Archives; p.18 ©CORBIS; p.20 ©Northwind Archives; p.23 ©NMPFT/SSPL/The Image Works; p.24l,r ©Library of Congress Prints & Photographs Div.; p.26 ©Library of Congress Prints & Photographs Div.; p.27 ©The Granger Collection; p.28 ©Associated Press/APWideWorld; p.31 ©Associated Press/APWideWorld; p.32 ©Associated Press/APWideWorld; p.36 ©Hulton Archive/Getty Images; p.39 ©Alexander Zemlianichenko/APWideWorld; p.40 ©John Gaps III/APWideWorld; p.47 ©Flip Schulke/CORBIS; p.48 ©The Granger Collection; p.49 ©Joseph Sohm/CORBIS; p.50 ©Jeff Chiu/APWideWorld; p.52 ©Dale Atkins/APWideWorld; p.53 ©Reuters/CORBIS; p.54 ©Wendell Metzen/Index Stock; p.56 ©Joseph Sohm/CORBIS; p.58 ©David Butow/CORBIS; p.62 ©Courtesy Baton Rouge Advocate; p.64 ©Bettmann/CORBIS; p.65 ©Bettmann/CORBIS; p.66 ©Bill Bachmann/Alamy Images; p.69 ©Flip Schulke/CORBIS; p.73 ©Tribune Media Services; p.75 ©Gina Martin/Getty Images; p.82 ©Gina Martin/Getty Images; p.101 ©Bridgeman Art Library/Getty Images; p.102 ©Yann Arthus-Bertrand/CORBIS; p.10 ©Bob Elsdale/Getty Images; p.104 ©David Barnes/Getty Images; p.107 ©Bridgeman Art Library/Getty Images; p.108t ©Edimedia/CORBIS; p.108b ©Bridgeman Art Library/Getty Images; p.110 ©Bridgeman Art Library/Getty Images; p.111 ©Hulton Archive/Getty Images; p.114 ©Bettmann/CORBIS; p.126r ©Tony Cordoza/Getty Images; p.126ml @British Museum, London, UK/Bridgeman Art Library; p.130 ©Najlah Feanny/CORBIS; p.131 ©John Coletti/Index Stock; p.149 Clay Bennett/©The Christian Science Monitor. All rights reserved.

Additional photography by Chris Hellier/CORBIS; Photos.com; Royalty-Free/CORBIS; Royalty free/Getty Images.

ILLUSTRATION

Bill Petersen p.60. All other art created by Element, LLC.

This product contains proprietary property of MapQuest, Inc.
Unauthorized use, including copying, of this product is expressly prohibited.

ISBN 1-4190-0800-5

Building Strategies is a registered trademark of Harcourt Achieve.

© 2006 Harcourt Achieve Inc.

All rights reserved. No part of the material protected by this copyright may be reproduced or utilized in any form or by any means, in whole or in part, without permission in writing from the copyright owner. Requests for permission should be mailed to: Paralegal Department, 6277 Sea Harbor Drive, Orlando, Florida 32887.

Steck-Vaughn is a trademark of Harcourt Achieve Inc.

Printed in the United States of America.

7 8 9 10 11 1421 15 14 13 12 11 10
4500271791

Contents

To the Learner

Congratulations! You have taken an important step as a lifelong learner. You have made the important decision to improve your reading skills. Read below to find out how Steck-Vaughn *Building Strategies for GED Success: Social Studies* will help you do just that.

- Take the **Pretest** on pages 3–9. Find out which skills you already know and which ones you need to practice. Mark them on the **Skills Preview Chart** on page 10.

- Study the five units in the book. Learn about U.S. and world history, civics and government, geography, and economics. Check out the **GED Tips**—they've got lots of helpful information.

- Complete the **GED Skill Reviews** and **GED Strategy Reviews**. You'll learn a lot of important reading, thinking, and test-taking skills.

- As you work through the book, use the **Answers and Explanations** at the back of the book to check your own work. Study the explanations to have a greater understanding of the concepts. You can also use the **Glossary** on page 151 when you want to check the meaning of a word.

- Review what you've learned by taking the **Posttest** on pages 143–149. Use the **Skills Review Chart** on page 150 to see the progress you've made!

Setting Goals

A goal is something you want to achieve. It's important to set goals in life to help you get what you want. It's also important to set goals for learning. So think carefully about what your goal is. Setting clear goals is an important part of your success. Choose your goal from those listed below. You may have more than one goal. If you don't see your goal, write it on the line.

My social studies goal is to

- get my GED
- improve my job skills
- get a new job that uses social studies

_____

A goal can take a long time to complete. To make achieving your goal easier, you can break your goal into small steps. By focusing on one step at a time, you are able to move closer and closer to achieving your goal.

Steps to your goals can include

- understanding social studies vocabulary
- reading newspaper articles about politics and the economy
- reading magazines that discuss world issues
- helping your children with their social studies homework

We hope that what you learn in this book will help you reach all of your goals.

Now, take the _Social Studies Pretest_ on pages 3–9. This will help you know what skills you need to improve so that you can reach your goals.

Social Studies Pretest

This pretest will give you an idea of the kind of work that you will be doing in this book. It will help you find out which social studies skills you are good at and which skills you need to improve. You will read short paragraphs, graphs, maps, and cartoons. You will also answer multiple-choice questions. There is no time limit.

Read each passage and question carefully. Circle the number of the correct answer.

Questions 1–2 are based on the following graph.

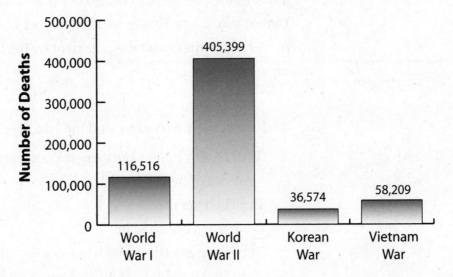

U.S. Casualties in Major 20th Century Wars

1. How many U.S. casualties were there in the Vietnam War?

   (1) 36,574
   (2) 58,209
   (3) 116,516
   (4) 405,399

2. How did U.S. deaths in World War II compare to U.S. deaths in World War I?

   (1) There were over triple the deaths in World War II.
   (2) There were twice as many deaths in World War II.
   (3) There were half as many deaths in World War II.
   (4) There were about the same number of deaths in both wars.

Questions 3–5 are based on the following passage.

There are three branches of the U.S. government. The legislative branch, or Congress, makes laws. The executive branch, headed by the president, carries out the laws. The judicial branch, including the Supreme Court, decides whether laws agree with the Constitution.

The U.S. government works on a system of "checks and balances." Each branch of government checks, or limits, the power of the other two branches. For example, the president has the power to appoint judges, or justices, to the Supreme Court. However, Congress can check this power of the president. That is because Congress must approve the president's choices of justices. Otherwise, the justices cannot take office. Finally, Supreme Court justices can check the power of Congress and the president by declaring that new laws are unconstitutional.

3. How are the executive and judicial branches different?
    (1) The Supreme Court carries out the laws; the president makes the laws.
    (2) The executive branch makes laws, and the judicial branch carries out the law.
    (3) The executive branch carries out the law, and the judicial branch decides matters of law.
    (4) The executive branch decides matters of law, and the judicial branch makes laws.

4. Three of these statements are facts. Choose the one that is an opinion.

    (1) Supreme Court justices are appointed by the president.
    (2) Congress must approve judges that the president chooses for the Supreme Court before they can take office.
    (3) The president should talk to leaders of Congress before choosing a Supreme Court justice.
    (4) The system of checks and balances limits the power of each of the branches of government.

5. What can you conclude from this passage?

   (1) The legislative branch is the most powerful of the three branches of government.
   (2) The president and Congress will always agree on appointments to the Supreme Court.
   (3) The president can control the actions of Congress and the Supreme Court.
   (4) The president, Congress, and the Supreme Court may not always agree.

Question 6 is based on the following circle graph.

The U.S. House of Representatives, 2005–2007

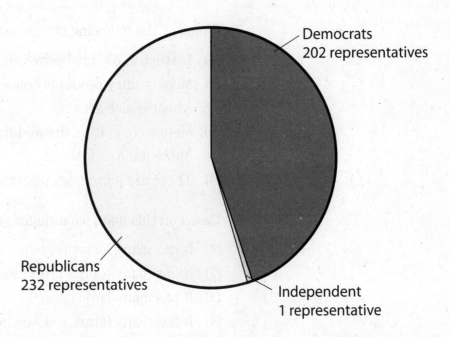

Democrats
202 representatives

Republicans
232 representatives

Independent
1 representative

6. Which political party held the majority in the U.S. House of Representatives during the years shown on the graph?

   (1) Republicans
   (2) Democrats
   (3) Independents
   (4) No party had a majority.

Questions 7–9 are based on the following map.

Farm, Forest, and Mining Products of Montana

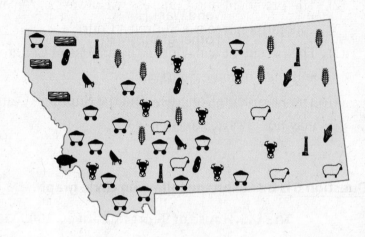

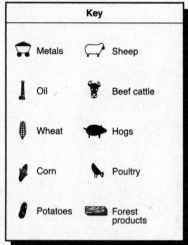

7. Which of the following statements is true?

    (1) Lettuce and strawberries are grown in Montana.
    (2) Most poultry products come from areas where wheat is also grown.
    (3) Metals come from the middle and western parts of Montana.
    (4) There are more hogs than beef cattle in Montana.

8. Based on this map, what might you conclude about Montana?

    (1) It has many factories.
    (2) It has many tourist attractions.
    (3) It has many large cities.
    (4) It has many farms and ranches.

9. What can you infer from this map?

    (1) People in the lumber business make more money than ranchers.
    (2) Montana is rich in resources.
    (3) Mining is dangerous and dirty.
    (4) Helena is the capital of Montana.

Questions 10–12 are based on the following passage.

In 1933, Adolf Hitler and his Nazi party came to power in Germany. Hitler wanted to make Germany powerful again. Germany had suffered after losing World War I. Hitler blamed Germany's problems on the Jews and other groups.

Hitler wanted to take over eastern Europe to expand Germany's territory. He invaded Poland in September 1939. England and France agreed to help Poland. Italy agreed to fight on Germany's side. This was the beginning of World War II.

The United States stayed out of the war until December 7, 1941. That was when Japan bombed a U.S. naval base in Pearl Harbor, Hawaii. Then the United States declared war against Japan. Later, Germany and Italy declared war against the United States, too.

Germany surrendered on May 6, 1945. Three months later, the United States dropped atomic bombs on two Japanese cities. Soon after, the Japanese surrendered and World War II ended.

10. What can you infer about Hitler's invasion of Poland?
    (1) Hitler wanted to expand German territory.
    (2) Hitler wanted to free Poland from a dictator.
    (3) Hitler wanted to help Japan.
    (4) Hitler wanted to help Italy.

11. Why did the United States enter World War II?
    (1) Atomic bombs were dropped on Japan.
    (2) Germany invaded Poland.
    (3) Germany surrendered.
    (4) Japan attacked Pearl Harbor.

12. When did World War II end?
    (1) when Germany surrendered
    (2) when Japan surrendered
    (3) before the U.S. dropped atomic bombs
    (4) on December 7, 1941

Questions 13–14 are based on the following graph.

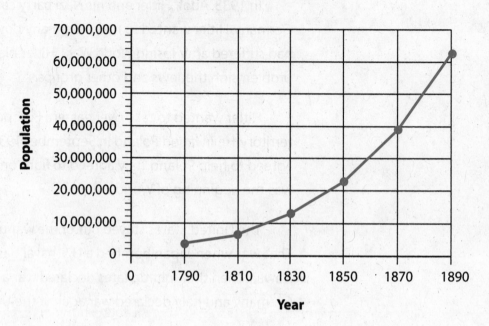

U.S. Population, 1790–1890

13. What was the population of the United States in 1790?

  (1) 4,000,000

  (2) 10,000,000

  (3) 13,000,000

  (4) 21,000,000

14. Based on the graph, what can you conclude about the U.S. population during this period?

  (1) The U.S. population grew very rapidly at first and then more slowly.

  (2) The U.S. population fell steadily.

  (3) The U.S. population grew slowly at first and then very rapidly.

  (4) Immigration caused the U.S. population to grow.

Questions 15–16 are based on the following cartoon.

THE CHRISTIAN SCIENCE MONITOR

15. What does this cartoon show?

   (1) an American farmer with many loans
   (2) the nation being buried by the money it owes
   (3) the credit card debt of American consumers
   (4) a budget surplus for the U.S. government

16. Which statement best expresses the cartoonist's opinion?

   (1) Farmers often have to go into debt.
   (2) The United States borrows money to pay for its expenses.
   (3) It is very difficult to pay off credit card debt.
   (4) A large national debt is difficult to keep up with.

When you have finished the *Social Studies Pretest*, check your answers on page 156. Then look at the chart on page 10.

Skills Preview Chart

This chart shows you which social studies skills you need to study. Check your answers. In the first column, circle the number of any questions you missed. Then look across the row to find out which skills you should review as well as the page numbers on which you can find instruction on those skills.

Questions	Skill	Pages
12	Understanding Time Order	20–21
2, 3	Comparing and Contrasting	30–31
13	Reading Line Graphs	36–37
11	Understanding Cause and Effect	56–57
15	Understanding Political Cartoons	62–63
4, 16	Recognizing Facts and Opinions	68–69
7	Reading Maps	80–81
9, 10	Making Inferences	90–91
1	Reading Bar Graphs	118–119
5, 8, 14	Drawing Conclusions	130–131
6	Reading Circle Graphs	136–137

pilgrim

In this unit you will learn about

- the early exploration of America
- how the United States became a nation
- the Civil War
- the Great Depression
- the Cold War
- how the Cold War ended

New Deal

civil rights

democracy

History is the study of past events. It includes the study of how countries are formed. In this unit, you will study how the United States became a country.

List two other countries.

_____

_____

U.S. history tells us about wars and hard times. It also tells us about hope, freedom, and democracy for all.

Citizens of the United States have certain rights, like the right to free speech. List another right U.S. citizens have.

_____

_____

Lesson 1

Europeans Explore America

fifteenth century
the years from 1401 to 1500

trade
to exchange goods for other goods

merchant
person who buys and sells things

route
way

settle
to make home

A fifteenth-century ship

Before the late **fifteenth century**, Europeans didn't know about the continents of North and South America. At that time, Europeans **traded** goods with people in India and China. The **merchants** had to travel by land. These trips were hard, and they often took many years. A trip by ship would have been much easier and faster. However, nobody knew an easy sea **route** to the east.

Christopher Columbus was an Italian explorer. Columbus thought he could reach India by sailing west. The queen of Spain paid for his trip. Spain hoped to increase its trade by finding a sea route to India.

Columbus started his trip in 1492. It lasted about three months. He landed on an island in the Bahamas, far from India. But Columbus was so sure that he had reached an island near India, he called this land the "Indies."

Columbus made three more trips. He explored part of South America and the islands of Cuba, Puerto Rico, and Jamaica. Columbus never found any riches. When he died, Columbus didn't know how important his trips had been.

Other Europeans explored and **settled** this part of the world. They called the continents of North and South America the "New World."

In 1498, a Portuguese explorer named Vasco da Gama reached India by sea. Unlike Columbus, da Gama sailed east. Later, Portuguese explorer Ferdinand Magellan tried to sail around the world. Magellan was killed in the Philippines. A small number of his men finished the trip.

Long before the Europeans arrived, millions of Native Americans were already living in the Americas. There were the Aztecs in Mexico and the Incas in Peru. The Aztecs built beautiful cities and had many riches. The Incas built a large system of roads between their cities.

In 1521, Spanish **conquistador** Hernando Cortez conquered the Aztecs. Later, Spain conquered the Incas, too. The Spanish took great amounts of gold from these lands. They also killed or made slaves of thousands of Native Americans.

conquistador
Spanish word for
conqueror, or someone
who defeats
someone else

An Aztec temple

claim
to take ownership

Northwest Passage
a sea route through North America to Asia

colony
a group of people who settle in one country but are governed by the parent country

GED Tip

Many GED passages explain historical events in time order. Pay attention to the sequence of events. Look for clue words such as *at first* and *finally*.

Spain and Portugal decided to divide the Americas between them. They said that no other country could **claim** land there. Other European countries disagreed. They wanted to find a **Northwest Passage** through North America to India. They also wanted land and gold for themselves.

France sent Jacques Cartier to North America to look for gold, as well as the Northwest Passage. He landed in Canada near the mouth of the St. Lawrence River. He claimed the area for France. Later, France started a trade **colony** at Quebec.

In the late 1500s, England sent Sir Humphrey Gilbert to find the Northwest Passage. Gilbert sailed to Newfoundland, an island off the coast of Canada. He claimed the island for England. Neither Gilbert nor any other explorer ever found the Northwest Passage. It doesn't exist.

Another Englishman, Sir Francis Drake, reached San Francisco Bay. Drake claimed this part of California for England. The English also started settlements in Virginia.

The Dutch set up a fur-trading post on the island of Manhattan. They named it New Amsterdam after the largest city in Holland.

Where Place Names Come From

Texas was once part of Mexico. As a result, many places in Texas have Spanish names.

Look at a map of where you live or a place that interests you. You may see names that look like words in other languages. You may see places named after places in other countries.

Practice

Vocabulary ■ **Write the word or words that best complete each sentence.**

1. A person who buys, sells, or trades goods is called a
   _____ .

2. Spain and Portugal decided to _____
   all the land in North and South America.

3. Hernando Cortez was a Spanish _____
   who took over the land of the Aztecs.

4. Europeans searched for the _____ , or
   a sea route through North America to Asia.

claim

colony

conquistador

merchant

Northwest Passage

Finding Facts ■ **Circle the number of the correct answer.**

5. European countries wanted to find a sea route to India and
   China because

   (1) they wanted to see if the world was round.
   (2) they could not get there by land.
   (3) a trip by ship would be easier and faster.
   (4) they hoped to find North and South America.

Finding Facts ■ **Write your answer to each question on the lines below.**

6. Which Native American group built a vast system of roads?

   _____

7. What did Columbus name the islands that he sailed to in 1492?

   _____

Check your answers on page 158.

Lesson 2   From Colonies to States

found
to start or establish

trading post
a store set up by merchants or traders

Pilgrims
a religious group that settled the Plymouth Colony

debtor
a person who owes money and can't pay it back

England wanted to **found** colonies to expand trade. English colonies like Jamestown (settled in 1607) and Massachusetts Bay (settled in 1628) were set up as **trading posts**. The trading posts were owned by merchants in England. These merchants wanted to sell goods to the colonies.

The Plymouth Colony in Massachusetts was founded by the **Pilgrims**. In England, the government protected only one religion, the Church of England. The Pilgrims left England because they wanted to be free to practice their own religion.

The Pilgrims sailed from England to North America in a ship called the *Mayflower*. They made a living by farming and also by selling animal skins to European traders.

The English government used the colonies to solve problems in England. **Debtors** and people who disagreed with the government were sent from England to the colonies.

The colonists traded with the Indians.

The Thirteen Colonies

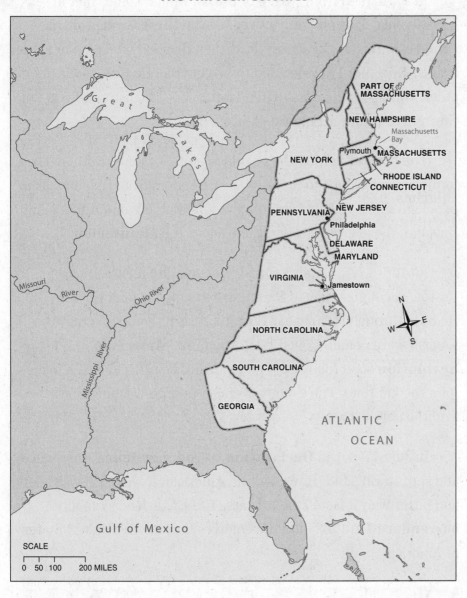

The Thirteen Colonies map showing:
PART OF MASSACHUSETTS, NEW HAMPSHIRE, Massachusetts Bay, Plymouth, MASSACHUSETTS, NEW YORK, RHODE ISLAND, CONNECTICUT, NEW JERSEY, PENNSYLVANIA, Philadelphia, DELAWARE, MARYLAND, VIRGINIA, Jamestown, NORTH CAROLINA, SOUTH CAROLINA, GEORGIA, ATLANTIC OCEAN, Great Lakes, Missouri River, Ohio River, Mississippi River, Gulf of Mexico

SCALE
0 50 100   200 MILES

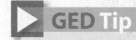

▶ **GED Tip**

Some GED Social Studies Test questions refer to maps. Look at the map. Pay attention to the title and the names of places.

By the 1700s, there were thirteen English colonies in North America. Life in the colonies was hard. The colonists worked for the **governor** of the colony. The governor worked with English merchants. The governor and the merchants became rich, but the colonists were poor, in spite of their hard work. Colonists weren't even allowed to own land or their own homes. However, the laws changed, and eventually, colonists could own land.

As the colonies grew larger and richer, the colonists wanted more freedom. They were angry because the English government raised the taxes it charged on some products. The colonists felt they had the right to set their own taxes.

governor
a person who rules an area such as a colony or a state

First Continental Congress
the first formal meeting to discuss problems the colonists had with England

boycott
to protest a government or any other group by refusing to use or buy its goods

Minutemen
civilians who were ready to fight at any time

American Revolution
the war between the colonists and the English government (1775–1783)

Declaration of Independence
the colonies' formal announcement of freedom from the English government

surrender
to give up to an enemy

In 1774, men from twelve of the thirteen colonies met in Philadelphia. This meeting was called the **First Continental Congress**. At this Congress, these men decided on a plan of action against England. They decided to **boycott** all English goods. In other words, the colonists agreed not to buy English products until England treated the colonists fairly.

The boycott helped the colonists unite, or join together. They formed small groups to fight for their freedom from England. The people in these groups were ready to fight at any minute. In New England, these groups called themselves the **Minutemen**.

In April 1775, English soldiers moved into an area near Boston. A colonist named Paul Revere made his famous ride. He rode through towns near Boston to warn the people that the English were coming. The first battle of the **American Revolution** soon followed. The following month, Congress met for a second time. The Congress chose George Washington to lead the colonial army.

In July 1776, the **Declaration of Independence** was signed and sent to England. However, the American Revolution was a long and bitter war. It lasted eight years. The English army finally **surrendered** in 1783, and the colonies became the United States of America.

General George Washington led the colonial army.

Practice

Vocabulary ■ **Write the word or words that best complete each sentence.**

1. _____, or people who owed money, settled in the English colonies.

2. Groups of colonists who could be ready to fight quickly were called the _____.

3. The war between the colonists and England was called the _____.

4. After the English army _____, the war was over.

> American Revolution
>
> debtors
>
> Minutemen
>
> Pilgrims
>
> surrendered

Finding Facts ■ **Circle the number of the correct answer.**

5. The Pilgrims left England because they

   (1)   wanted to get rich in the colonies.

   (2)   wanted to be free to practice their religion.

   (3)   were debtors.

   (4)   were merchants.

6. The colonists became angry because England

   (1)   raised taxes on some products.

   (2)   traded with the colonies.

   (3)   boycotted the colonists' goods.

   (4)   sent debtors to the colonies.

Finding Facts ■ **Write your answer to each question on the lines below.**

7. What was signed in July 1776?

   _____

8. Whom did the colonists choose to lead their army?

   _____

Check your answers on page 158.

Understanding Time Order

When you study history, it helps to know the order in which events happened. You need to be able to recognize the sequence, or order, of events.

Dates and times can help you recognize time order, and so can key words like *before, after,* and *later.* The examples below show time order.

- Columbus began his voyage in <u>1492</u>.
- <u>Six years after</u> Columbus's first voyage, Vasco da Gama reached India by sailing east.
- <u>Before</u> the Europeans came, the Aztecs had built great cities in Mexico.

 Strategy Read the passage. Ask yourself: Are there clue words for time order? What are they?

1. Look for general time clues. These include words like *before, after, first, second, soon, then, later,* and *finally.*

2. Look for specific time clues. These include words that name days (Tuesday), dates (April 2), years (1836), or times (1:00 P.M.).

Exercise 1: Read the paragraph. Underline key time order words or phrases.

In 1492, Christopher Columbus began his first trip across the Atlantic Ocean in search of India. After that first trip, he went back three more times. When he died in 1505, he still had not found a route to India. It wasn't until much later that people realized the importance of his trips.

Sometimes passages don't have time order words.

 Strategy Look for key events or actions. Ask yourself: Are events listed in the order in which they happened?

1. Identify important events as you read.

2. Read carefully to see whether events are listed in the order in which they happened.

Exercise 2: Read the following paragraphs. Which one is in time order? Circle the number of the correct answer.

1. There are two reasons Europeans wanted to find a sea route to India. They needed India's silk, jewels, and other goods. They thought that land travel took too long.

2. For seven years, Columbus tried to find someone to pay for his trips. He asked John II of Portugal. He wrote to Henry VI of England. He met with Spain's Queen Isabella.

Exercise 3: Rewrite the paragraph you chose in Exercise 2. Begin each sentence with a key word such as *first, then, after,* or *finally.*

_____

_____

_____

_____

_____

_____

_____

Check your answers on page 158.

Lesson 3 The Civil War

In the United States during the 1850s, the way of life in the North was different from the way of life in the South. One important difference was slavery. Many white people in the South owned black slaves. There were very few slaves in the North.

The main business in the South was farming. Cotton, sugar cane, and tobacco were grown on very large farms. These farms were called **plantations**. Many people were needed to work on the plantations. It was cheaper for the plantation owners to use slaves than to pay workers who were not slaves.

There were farms in the North, but they were usually small. The main business in the North was **manufacturing**. Many people worked in factories instead of on farms. Many people in the North spoke out against slavery. Some helped slaves escape from the plantations and move to the North.

plantation
a large farm on which crops are raised

manufacturing
making products, usually in factories

Northern and Southern States in the Civil War

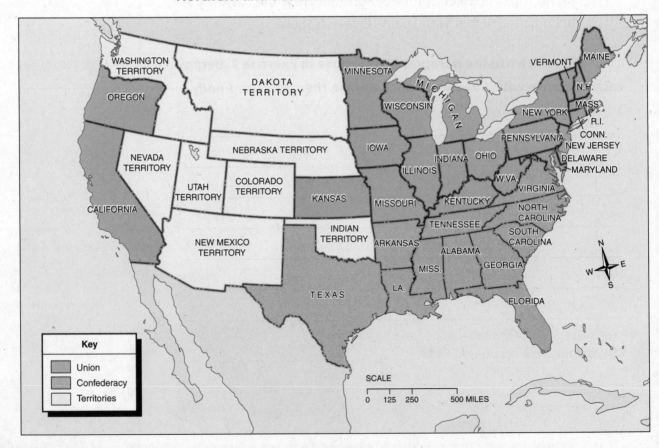

Key
- Union
- Confederacy
- Territories

SCALE
0 125 250 500 MILES

Disagreement between the North and South over slavery grew over time. New parts of the United States were being settled. When new states joined the United States, each state had to **declare** itself either a **free state** or a slave state. The North did not want more slave states, and the South did not want more free states.

In 1860, Abraham Lincoln was elected president. He had spoken out against slavery, so seven Southern states protested his election. They **seceded** from the United States and set up a new country. They called this country the Confederate States of America, or the **Confederacy**. Four more states eventually seceded. The territories in the United States were on the side of the **Union**.

Fighting broke out between the Confederacy and the Union in the spring of 1861. This was the beginning of the American **Civil War**. Most of the battles of the Civil War took place in the South.

The Union had many advantages in the war. The Union had factories to make guns, cannons, boots, and other war supplies. The Union also controlled most of the railroads. The railroads were important for getting soldiers and supplies to the battles. The Confederacy had problems getting supplies to its soldiers. The Confederate soldiers had one advantage, though. They were fighting the war on their own land.

declare
to say publicly

free state
any state where slavery wasn't allowed

secede
to leave a group or organization officially

Confederacy
the South during the Civil War

Union
the North during the Civil War

civil war
a war between two groups of people in the same country

Confederate soldiers' camp

Emancipation Proclamation
the document that stated all slaves would be free

segregation
social separation of different groups of people

President Lincoln wanted the Southern States to rejoin the Union, but he also wanted the slaves to be freed. In 1863, he signed the **Emancipation Proclamation**. The Emancipation Proclamation stated that all slaves would be freed.

The Civil War lasted four years. The Confederate army finally surrendered in 1865, and the war ended. The North and South were again one country. The cost to the country was high. Almost 600,000 people had died.

Nearly four million slaves were freed. New laws were passed to give black people the same rights as white people. However, **segregation** of blacks and whites lasted almost another hundred years.

President Lincoln signed the Emancipation Proclamation in 1863.

After the War, African Americans could attend school for the first time.

▶ **GED Tip**

Some GED Social Studies Test questions refer to photographs. Read the captions that go with photographs. They give important information.

Practice

Vocabulary ■ **Write the word or words that best complete each sentence.**

1. Slavery was not allowed in the _____.

2. Fighting between two groups in the same country is called _____.

civil war

free states

manufacturing

Understanding Time Order ■ **Circle the number of the correct answer.**

3. The Confederate States were formed

   (1) after seven Southern states seceded from the Union.
   (2) after Lincoln signed the Emancipation Proclamation.
   (3) after the Civil War.
   (4) after the slaves were freed.

4. President Lincoln signed the Emancipation Proclamation

   (1) before the Civil War began.
   (2) during the Civil War.
   (3) after the Confederacy surrendered.
   (4) during the 1850s.

Finding Facts ■ **Circle the number of the correct answer.**

5. The policy of segregation in the South lasted

   (1) until 1861.
   (2) until 1865.
   (3) for almost another hundred years after the Civil War.
   (4) until the Confederate states surrendered.

6. The Confederacy was made up of

   (1) slave states.
   (2) Union states.
   (3) free states.
   (4) Northern states.

Check your answers on page 158.

Lesson 4 The Great Depression

communicate
to talk with or share information with other people

boom
a time of rapid economic growth

profit
the amount of money a company has left after subtracting the cost of doing business

stock
a share that a person owns in a company

stock market
the place where stocks are bought and sold

depression
a long period of economic decline

The 1920s were a time of great change. New inventions changed people's lives. Cars and airplanes made travel faster and easier. The telephone and radio helped people **communicate** over long distances. Millions of people saw movies for the first time. Many parts of the United States got electric lights for the first time.

The 1920s were a **boom** time for businesses. Americans earned more money than ever before. Many businesses grew quickly and made large **profits**. Thousands of people bought **stocks** in big companies. Prices on the **stock market** went up as companies made larger and larger profits. People expected their stocks to make them rich quickly.

In October 1929, stock prices suddenly fell. Many people who owned stocks panicked and sold them. This made prices go down even more. On Tuesday, October 29, 1929, the stock market crashed, or failed. Owners of stocks lost 74 billion dollars. This day is remembered as Black Tuesday.

Banks closed. Many people lost their savings. Businesses closed, and people lost their jobs and their homes. A time of great hardship began. The United States went into a **depression**. Soon the depression spread to other countries. This time was called the Great Depression. During the worst of the Great Depression in the United States, one worker out of every four workers was unemployed.

People stood in bread lines to get food. Many people went hungry during the Great Depression.

American farmers suffered during this time. Prices for crops were low. On the Great Plains, dust storms and a long drought added to farmers' troubles. The soil blew away. Many acres of farmland became a wasteland. This area was nicknamed "the Dust Bowl." More than three million people left their farms in the 1930s. Many moved to California.

By 1932, many Americans were desperate. That year President Hoover ran for re-election. Hoover was very unpopular because he had not ended the Great Depression. He was not re-elected. Instead, Franklin D. Roosevelt was chosen to be the new president.

Roosevelt said the Great Depression was a national emergency and that he had a new plan to help the country. This plan was called the **New Deal**. The New Deal would get the economy growing. It would put Americans back to work.

Roosevelt had many ideas for the New Deal. He **proposed** new laws giving the government some control of the banks. He proposed other laws that helped factory workers. These laws set minimum wages and work hours. Farmers received government loans to start up their farms again.

New Deal
the programs and laws created by Roosevelt to get the U.S. economy out of the depression

propose
suggest

Many farm families packed up their cars and left the Dust Bowl.

GED Tip

When reading passages on the GED Social Studies Test, find the main idea of each paragraph.

Social Security
a government insurance program that pays retired and disabled workers and their families

Some New Deal programs gave people jobs. One program hired workers to build large projects such as dams and sewer systems. Another program paid young men to work in the national parks and forests.

The most important jobs program was the Works Progress Administration (WPA). This program hired 3.5 million workers. Most of the workers built hospitals, schools, and airports. Some WPA workers were writers, artists, and actors. They recorded what life was like during the Great Depression. They took photographs and painted pictures. They put on plays. They collected the stories and songs of the American people.

The government also started **Social Security** and an unemployment insurance program. Both of these programs still exist today. Many other laws were made to protect people and businesses. The Securities and Exchange Commission was formed to watch over stock trading. Roosevelt thought this would help prevent stock market crashes. He hoped the New Deal programs would prevent a Great Depression from ever happening again.

Eventually, the Great Depression did end. American companies began making machines and weapons for a huge war in Europe and Asia. By 1940, the economy was growing very rapidly.

The New Deal created jobs to help the economy.

Practice

Vocabulary ■ Write the word that best completes each sentence.

1. Buying a share of _____ in a company is a way to buy part of that business.

2. The price of stocks goes up quickly during a _____ .

3. As business failures spread to other countries in 1929, the world economy went into a _____ .

| boom |
| market |
| depression |
| stock |

Understanding Time Order ■ Circle the number of the correct answer.

4. The Great Depression started

    (1) after the stock market crash of 1929.
    (2) after Roosevelt proposed new laws giving government some control of the banks.
    (3) in the early 1920s.
    (4) after Roosevelt announced his New Deal.

5. Roosevelt was elected president

    (1) before the Great Depression started.
    (2) on Black Tuesday.
    (3) during the Great Depression.
    (4) after the Great Depression.

Finding Facts ■ Circle the number of the correct answer.

6. The WPA was a jobs program that

    (1) set minimum wages for workers.
    (2) watched over stock trading.
    (3) hired people to work on government projects.
    (4) provided unemployment insurance.

Check your answers on page 159.

Comparing and Contrasting

To compare means to show how one thing is like another. To contrast means to show how one thing is different from another. Comparing or contrasting events or time periods can help you understand history and see how the world has changed. The following sentences show comparisons and contrasts.

- "This grapefruit tastes <u>as</u> sweet as an orange," said Sharon.
- Jeff likes to be with people. <u>However</u>, Bill likes to be alone.
- "Life is almost the <u>same</u> here as it was in our old neighborhood," said Keith.

 Strategy   Read the paragraph. Ask yourself: Are there clue words that show comparison or contrast?

1. Look for clue words that show a comparison: *like, as, similar, same, best, worst, better, worse, less, more*
2. Look for clue words that show a contrast: *however, but, unlike, different, in contrast*

Exercise 1: Read the paragraph. Then answer the questions.

In the 1920s, businesses made large profits. The 1930s were not the same, however. Business failures were unlike anything they had ever been before. The depression was as bad for farmers as it was for people in the cities. Many farmers lost their farms or were barely able to grow enough to eat.

1. **List the word or words in the pargraph that show comparison.**

   _____

2. **List the word or words in the pargraph that show contrast.**

   _____

Strategy Look for key events or ideas. Ask yourself: Are these events or ideas being compared or contrasted?

1. Identify important events and ideas as you read.

2. Decide whether events or ideas are being compared (shown as being alike) or contrasted (shown as being different).

Exercise 2: Read the paragraph. Underline the things, ideas, and events being compared or contrasted. Circle the clue words.

Roosevelt's New Deal was like a rope thrown to drowning people. Government began to play a role in people's lives more than ever before. The government created a safety net to help protect Americans against hard times. Some Americans think Roosevelt was one of the best presidents the United States has ever had.

Exercise 3: Use the following information to write a paragraph comparing or contrasting the Great Depression with conditions of the U.S. economy today. Use clue words that show comparison and contrast.

Franklin D. Roosevelt

During the Great Depression, many people had no food and no place to live. About 13 million Americans had no jobs at the height of the depression.

_____

_____

_____

_____

_____

Check your answers on page 159.

Second World War
World War II, fought between England, the United States, the Soviet Union, and their allies on one side and Germany, Italy, Japan, and their allies on the other side (1939–1945)

public works
projects such as roads, bridges, and dams paid for by the government for the people's use

welfare
money given by the government to people who need help

consumer goods
goods that are made for people's needs and wants

After the war, factories that had made war supplies began to make consumer goods.

After winning the **Second World War** in 1945, the United States became the world's most powerful nation. During World War II, many cities in Europe were destroyed because major battles were fought there. Other major battles took place in Asia. Atomic bombs destroyed two Japanese cities in 1945. Atomic bombs are very powerful weapons. One bomb can destroy an entire city. The United States was the only country that had the atomic bomb.

Because of that destruction, the Europeans and Japanese had to rebuild their countries. They worked hard to rebuild their cities, factories, and farms.

The United States didn't have to rebuild. No battles had been fought on American soil. During the war, American factories had grown rapidly. These factories made ships, airplanes, and other supplies used to fight the war overseas.

The years after World War II were a time of economic growth in the United States. At first, not much was available for people to buy. Then the factories that had made war supplies started to make **consumer goods**, such as cars and home appliances. This started a business boom, or growth. It also created jobs for veterans, or soldiers returning from the war.

There was a boom in spending by the government, too. After the war, the government spent money on **public works**, health, education, and **welfare** programs. The government created a new program called the G.I. Bill. The G.I. Bill paid for veterans to go to college. It also gave them money to start new businesses. The G.I. Bill helped the U.S. economy to grow.

In the early 1950s, the United States worried about losing its place as the world's most powerful nation. During World War II, the Soviet Union and the United States had fought on the same side. But beginning in the 1950s, the United States felt threatened by the Soviets.

The Americans and Soviets had very different forms of government. Americans felt that the Soviet form of government was a threat to **democracy**. The Soviets wanted to spread **communism**, their type of government, to other countries. In 1949, they helped Communists take over China. In addition, the Soviet Union developed an atomic bomb.

The conflict between the United States and the Soviet Union was called the **Cold War**. That was because no fighting took place between them. However, the two countries built many powerful weapons. Soon each country had enough weapons to destroy the other.

In 1957, the Soviet Union sent the first **satellite**, *Sputnik 1*, into space. A month later they sent up *Sputnik 2*. Americans thought that if the Soviets could build satellites, they could also make better weapons. Americans wanted the government to spend money developing and building new weapons and to equip, train, and pay soldiers.

The United States also moved ahead in space research. The United States sent the first American into space in 1961. In 1969, the United States sent the first person to the moon.

democracy
a form of government in which power is held by the people

communism
a system of government where the state controls industry and business, and all goods are shared equally by the people

Cold War
the struggle between the United States and the Soviet Union (end of World War II–1989)

satellite
an object sent into space to circle Earth

In 1969, Americans were the first to land on the moon.

After World War II, there was also a boom in population. Many returning soldiers wanted to start a family. During the 1950s, about 28 million American babies were born. This growth in population was called the **baby boom**.

The baby boom lasted from 1946 to 1965. During that time, the U.S. population grew by 75 million. The baby boom helped the country's economic growth because there were even more families buying American goods.

The baby boomers grew up during a time of plenty. But education became very important for getting a good job. Some World War II veterans had not finished high school. The GED (General Educational Development) Test was started to help these veterans get their high school diplomas. Many of the veterans' children became the first members of their families to go to college.

baby boom
a period of increased American births (1946–1965)

▶ **GED Tip**

GED passages may include unfamiliar words. Use nearby sentences to figure out what these words mean.

After the war, many Americans started families. The rise in population was called the baby boom.

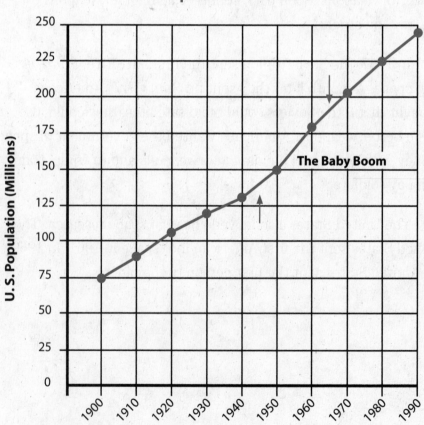

U. S. Population from 1900–1990

Practice

Vocabulary ■ Write the word that best completes each sentence.

1. _____ programs give money, food, housing, and health care to people who are in need.

2. In a country that practices _____, the government owns most of the businesses.

> boom
>
> communism
>
> welfare

Compare and Contrast ■ Circle the number of the correct answer.

3. During World War II, the United States and the Soviet Union fought on the same side. After the war,

   (1) the United States felt threatened by the Soviets.
   (2) they worked together to rebuild Europe and Japan.
   (3) the Soviet Union was no longer important.
   (4) the Soviet Union became the most powerful nation in the world.

Finding Facts ■ Circle the number of the correct answer.

4. After World War II, the Europeans and Japanese had to rebuild their countries because

   (1) they were forced to do so by the Americans.
   (2) they had strong economies.
   (3) their cities, factories, and farms had been destroyed.
   (4) they wanted to sell goods to each other.

5. Read the line graph on page 34. Between 1940 and 1970, there was a large increase in the U.S. population because

   (1) many people completed high school and went to college.
   (2) after the war, many Americans started families.
   (3) fewer Americans traveled to other countries.
   (4) the government asked people to have children.

Check your answers on page 159.

GED Skill Strategy

Reading Line Graphs

A line graph shows how something changes over time. You need to be able to understand what a line graph shows. You also need to be able to find specific information, or data, in a line graph.

The graph is made up of a vertical axis, or the line going up and down, and a horizontal axis, or the line going across. The title of a graph tells you what the graph shows. The labels tell you the specific data being shown.

▶ **Strategy** Look at the line graph. Ask yourself: What is the title? What do the labels say?

1. Look for the title. This is in large letters above the graph.

2. Read the labels. There are labels for the vertical axis. There are different labels on the horizontal axis.

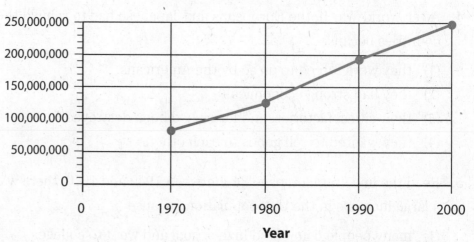

TV Sets in American Homes, 1970–2000

Exercise 1: Look at the graph above. Complete the sentences.

1. The vertical axis shows the number of _____ .

2. The horizontal axis shows the years from _____ to _____ .

▶ **Strategy**   Look at the line in the graph. Ask yourself:
Is the line going up or down? What does a dot on the
line mean?

1. See if the line goes up, goes down, or stays level. If
    the line goes up, there was an increase. If it goes
    down, there was a decrease. If it remains level, there
    was no change.

2. Figure out what a dot on the line means. Read up to
    the dot from the label on the horizontal axis. Then
    read across to the label on the vertical axis.

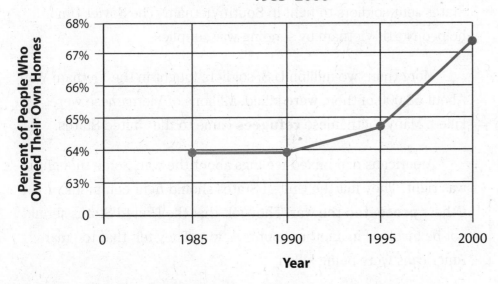

**People Who Owned Homes in the United States
1985–2000**

**Exercise 2: Look at the line graph above. Put a _T_ for true or an _F_
for false next to each statement.**

____ **1.**   The percent of people who owned their home stayed
    the same between 1985 and 1990.

____ **2.**   The percent of people who owned their home fell
    between 1990 and 1995.

____ **3.**   In the year 2000, almost 70 percent of people owned
    their home.

Check your answers on page 160.

During the Cold War, the United States and the Soviet Union never fought one another. However, they took sides in wars around the world. One of these wars was the Vietnam War.

Vietnam was divided into two parts. Communists held the northern part. Non-communists held the southern part. In 1957, communists in the south started fighting to change the government there. These **rebels** were called the Viet Cong. The North Vietnamese helped the rebels. This is how the Vietnam War started.

rebel
a person who fights against an established government or authority

The United States worried that the communists would win the Vietnam War. If that happened, some Americans thought that communism would spread to other countries. In 1965, the United States sent soldiers to fight in South Vietnam. The Soviet Union helped North Vietnam by sending war supplies.

refugees
people who flee a place because of disaster or war

More than two million U.S. soldiers fought in the Vietnam War. About 58,000 of them were killed. Millions of Vietnamese were killed. Many Vietnamese **refugees** came to the United States.

protest
to speak out against something

Americans had mixed feelings about the war. Some thought it was right. They felt the United States should fight communism. Others **protested** the war. They felt that the United States should not be involved in another country's war. They felt that too many Americans were being killed.

The United States pulled its troops out of Vietnam in 1973. In 1975, South Vietnam surrendered. North and South Vietnam were joined, forming a single communist nation. However, communism did not spread to any other countries in the region.

Vietnam 1954–1975

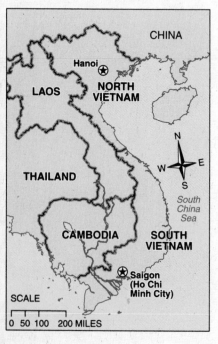

Other Cold War conflicts took place in Europe. After World War II, Europe was divided into communist and non-communist countries. Most countries in Eastern Europe were communist.

Germany was divided into communist East Germany and non-communist West Germany. Berlin, the old capital city, was a divided city. East Berlin was communist. West Berlin was non-communist.

In 1948, the Soviet Union tried to drive the United States and its allies out of West Berlin. It stopped all shipments of goods to West Berlin. The Soviets set up a **blockade**. The blockade of West Berlin caused food shortages there.

Soon, the United States and its allies began to fly food, fuel, and medicines into West Berlin. These supply flights were called an airlift. The Berlin airlift was a success. After a year, the Soviets ended the blockade of West Berlin.

Berlin remained a troubled city. Many people left communist East Berlin to move to West Berlin. In 1961, the East Germans built a wall around West Berlin. The Berlin Wall kept East Berliners from escaping to West Berlin.

People in Eastern Europe and the Soviet Union had very little freedom. Sometimes they did not even have enough food.

By the 1980s, some communist leaders thought it was time to make changes. Mikhail Gorbachev was one of those leaders. He was the president of the Soviet Union. Gorbachev allowed people to have more freedom. He also tried to improve the economy. Gorbachev's changes in the Soviet Union led to even more changes throughout Eastern Europe.

GED Tip

Some GED Social Studies Test passages contrast places. Look for pairs of sentences that tell how places differ from one another.

blockade
cutting off an area so that normal travel and trade cannot take place

Mikhail Gorbachev was a communist leader who made important changes in the Soviet Union.

revolt
to fight against authority

republic
a country whose leader is chosen by the people

reform
an effort to improve

In 1989, people from many of the countries in Eastern Europe **revolted** against their communist governments. Gorbachev did not try to stop these revolts. Communist governments in Hungary, Poland, and other countries fell. Democratic governments replaced them.

In November 1989, the German people tore down the Berlin Wall. The Berlin Wall had been an important symbol of the Cold War. The tearing down of the wall was a major step in ending the Cold War. In 1990, East Germany and West Germany united to become one non-communist nation.

The changes in Eastern Europe continued through the early 1990s. The East European country of Yugoslavia became separate **republics**. War broke out between groups that had once been part of the same country.

In 1991, Soviet leaders who did not like Gorbachev's **reforms** tried to force him out of office. They did not succeed, but their effort left Gorbachev with less power. Republics within the Soviet Union began demanding their freedom from Soviet rule. Led by Russia, some of these republics broke away from the Soviet Union and formed the Commonwealth of Independent States (C.I.S.). Gorbachev resigned, and the Soviet Union came to an end. When the Soviet Union fell apart, the Cold War was over.

In 1989, Germans tore down the Berlin Wall.

Practice

Vocabulary ■ Write the word that best completes each sentence.

1. Some Americans _____ the Vietnam War.

2. During a _____, there may be food shortages because normal trade is cut off.

3. Communist governments in many East European countries fell after people in those countries _____.

> blockade
> protested
> republic
> revolted

Time Order ■ Circle the number of the correct answer.

4. The Soviet Union came to an end

   (1) before the Cold War began.

   (2) when Gorbachev resigned from office.

   (3) when Gorbachev tried to make changes in the economy.

   (4) before the Berlin Wall was built.

5. After the Berlin Wall was torn down,

   (1) the Berlin airlift ended.

   (2) communism fell in East Germany.

   (3) the Germans rebuilt it.

   (4) East and West Germany were divided.

Finding Facts ■ Circle the number of the correct answer.

6. The Soviet Union helped North Vietnam during the Vietnam War by

   (1) taking over its government.

   (2) sending soldiers to South Vietnam.

   (3) sending war supplies.

   (4) setting up a blockade of South Vietnam.

Check your answers on page 160.

Previewing Test Questions

On the GED Social Studies Test, you will answer questions based on passages and illustrations, or graphics. One way to answer GED questions is to preview the questions. That means you read the questions before you read the passage or study the graphic. This helps you look for clues to help you answer the questions.

 Strategy Try the strategy on the example below. Use these steps.

Step 1 Read the question. What is it asking you to find out?

Step 2 Read the paragraph. Look for the information the question asks for.

Step 3 Answer the question.

In 1914, World War I began in Europe. At first, the United States did not take sides. But Germany sank passenger ships crossing the Atlantic Ocean. When Germany sank the *Lusitania* in 1915, 128 Americans died. In 1916, Germany said it would stop attacking passenger ships. But in 1917, Germany began the attacks again. On April 2, 1917, the United States entered World War I, going to war with Germany.

What happened shortly after Germany sank the *Lusitania*?

(1) World War I started in Europe.

(2) The United States said that it would not take sides in the war.

(3) The United States entered World War II.

(4) Germany said it would stop sinking passenger ships.

In Step 1 you read the question. It asked what took place shortly after Germany sank the *Lusitania*. In Step 2 you read the paragraph and studied the order of events. In Step 3 you answered the question. The correct answer is (4). Germany said it would stop sinking passenger ships. Choices (1) and (2) took place earlier. Choice (3) took place about 25 years later.

Practice the strategy. Use the steps you learned. Circle the number of the correct answer.

England, Spain, and France established colonies in North America during the 1500s and 1600s. The English built towns and farms on the east coast. The Spanish built forts and towns in Florida, California, and the Southwest. The French built fur-trading posts. Unlike the English and Spanish, the French had few towns and settlers.

1. Based on the paragraph, how did French colonies differ from English and Spanish colonies?

   (1) The French colonies were in North America.
   (2) The French colonies were established in the 1500s and 1600s.
   (3) The French had few colonists and towns.
   (4) The French colonies were in the Southwest.

Check your answers on page 160.

Read each paragraph and question carefully. Circle the number of the correct answer.

Questions 1–3 are based on the following paragraph.

George Washington became the first U.S. president on April 30, 1789. After he made his first speech to lawmakers in Congress, they argued about how to address Washington. Some lawmakers liked "His Most Benign Highness." Some liked "His Highness, the President of the United States." But most people were angered by these titles. They thought such titles had no place in a democracy. Congress finally settled on "Mr. President," the title we use to this day.

1. Which event happened first?

   (1) Washington spoke to Congress.

   (2) Congress had a disagreement about Washington's title.

   (3) Washington was elected president.

   (4) Congress addressed Washington as "Mr. President."

2. What happened right after Washington's speech?

   (1) Congress met for the first time.

   (2) Congress discussed how to address Washington.

   (3) Congress replied to Washington's speech.

   (4) The nation became a democracy.

3. How are the titles "His Most Benign Highness" and "His Highness, the President of the United States" different from the title "Mr. President"?

   (1) They are more formal than "Mr. President."

   (2) They are more democratic than "Mr. President."

   (3) More lawmakers liked those titles than "Mr. President."

   (4) They are easier to say than "Mr. President."

Questions 4–6 are based on the following graph.

U. S. Slave Population from 1800–1860

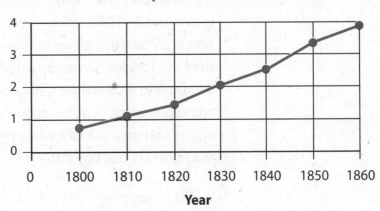

4. Approximately how many slaves lived in the United States in 1860?

   (1) 2 million
   (2) 3 million
   (3) 4 million
   (4) more than 4 million

5. When was the slave population of the United States just over 1 million?

   (1) before 1800
   (2) in 1810
   (3) in 1820
   (4) after 1830

6. How did the size of the slave population in the United States change during the period shown on the graph?

   (1) It increased.
   (2) It decreased.
   (3) It increased and then it decreased.
   (4) It decreased and then it increased.

Questions 7–8 are based on the following paragraph.

The actions of many individuals helped African Americans win their rights. In 1947, Jackie Robinson became the first African American baseball player in the major leagues. In 1951, Oliver Brown sued the Topeka, Kansas, Board of Education. He wanted to send his daughter to an all-white school near their home. His victory helped end segregation in public schools. In 1955, Rosa Parks refused to give up her seat on a bus to a white passenger. Her arrest led to the 1956 Montgomery bus boycott.

7. What happened after Rosa Parks was arrested?

    (1) She refused to give up her seat on a bus.

    (2) Jackie Robinson joined a major league baseball team.

    (3) Oliver Brown sued the school board in Topeka, Kansas.

    (4) The Montgomery bus boycott began.

8. All three African Americans mentioned in the paragraph

    (1) ended segregation in public schools.

    (2) boycotted white businesses.

    (3) sent their children to all-white schools.

    (4) wanted to be treated as equals.

Check your answers on page 160.

Unit 1 Skill Check-Up Chart

Check your answers. In the first column, circle the numbers of any questions that you missed. Then look across the rows to see the skills you need to review and the pages where you can find each skill.

Question	Skill	Page
1, 2, 7	Understanding Time Order	20–21
3, 8	Comparing and Contrasting	30–31
4, 5, 6	Reading Line Graphs	36–37

Unit 2

Civics and Government

In this unit you will learn about

- the U.S. Constitution
- the three branches of government
- how presidents are elected
- the movement for civil rights

boycott

Congress

ratify

poll

The study of civics and government includes learning about the rights of citizens and about the U.S. government. In this unit, you will learn how our government works.

Write something that you know about the U.S. government.

_____

_____

Civics and government also involves learning about elections. You will learn how political candidates are chosen and what happens in elections.

Write something that you know about the last presidential election.

_____

_____

government
the method of running a country, state, or city

representative
a person who voices the needs, wants, and opinions of a group of people

federal government
a central, national government

Constitution
the document that sets forth the laws of the United States

After the American Revolution, the thirteen states were united by a weak **government**. This government had many problems. In 1787, each state sent **representatives** to a meeting to solve these problems. These representatives decided the states needed a strong **federal government**. The representatives wrote a new plan of government. They called this plan the **Constitution**. Many heroes of the Revolution, like George Washington and Benjamin Franklin, helped write the Constitution. The Constitution became law in 1788.

The American Constitution is based on certain beliefs. One belief is that government gets its power from the people. People elect, or choose, their lawmakers. Another belief is that government and religion should be separated. People may practice any religion they wish, and the government does not favor any particular religion. Another belief is that both the federal government and state governments have rights.

The Constitution was signed in Philadelphia on September 17, 1787.

The writers of the Constitution had to make some **compromises**. Some of the writers felt that the federal government should be very strong. Others were afraid that the federal government might have too much power. The federal government was given the power to print money, run the post office, control the armed forces, direct trade between the states, and declare war. The states were given powers, too.

Controlling the power of the federal government was important. So, the Constitution split the federal government into three **branches**. That way, each branch could keep the other two branches from becoming too powerful.

The Constitution set up a plan of government that still works today. The Constitution has a preamble, or introduction, and seven **articles**. All new laws must follow the Constitution.

compromise
an agreement in which each side gives up something

branch
a part or section

article
a section of the Constitution

amendment
a change or addition

The Preamble to the Constitution with part of the first article

The first three articles of the Constitution give different powers to Congress, the president, and the courts. Article Four is about states' rights. Article Five tells how to make changes to the Constitution. Article Six makes the Constitution and federal laws more powerful than state laws. The last article says that the Constitution became law when nine states accepted it.

The writers of the Constitution knew the government would have to change as the country grew. They allowed for additions, or **amendments**, to the Constitution. There have been 27 amendments to the Constitution.

GED Tip

Some GED Social Studies questions refer to the Constitution. Be sure you understand what the Constitution says.

Bill of Rights
the part of the Constitution that lists people's rights

majority rule
when more than half of the people agree on the laws of government

press
news that is published in newspapers, magazines, radio, television or on the Internet

censorship
the act of preventing people from expressing their views

The first ten amendments are called the **Bill of Rights**. The Bill of Rights gives many rights to the people. It limits the powers of the federal government. Certain rights are also given to the states. The Constitution is based on **majority rule**. Yet the rights of people who disagree with the majority are also protected.

Some of the amendments in the Bill of Rights give people rights that many Americans take for granted. For example, the First Amendment allows freedom of the **press**. Some people believe that this includes freedom from **censorship** of any kind. Other people disagree.

An important right that people have is the right to vote. A citizen must be 18 years old to vote. The 15th, 19th, and 26th amendments are about voting rights.

The Constitution is more than two hundred years old, but it is still a useful plan of government. It protects the rights of the individual. At the same time, it provides a strong central government. The Constitution also allows for change and growth in government. This is important because society itself changes.

Free speech is protected by the First Amendment of the Bill of Rights.

Practice

Vocabulary ■ **Write the word that best completes each sentence.**

1. Preventing people from expressing their views is
   _____ .

2. The _____ is a document that is a plan
   of government.

3. The Constitution can be changed with _____ .

amendments
articles
Constitution
censorship

Understanding Time Order ■ **Put these sentences in the proper
time order. Write *first, second*, and *third*.**

_____ **4.** The Bill of Rights was added to the Constitution.

_____ **5.** Representatives met in 1787 to write the Constitution.

_____ **6.** The Constitution became law in 1788.

Finding Facts ■ **Circle the number of the correct answer.**

7. The American Constitution is based on which belief?

   (1) People of a country should have the power to make their
   own laws.

   (2) Government should have unlimited power.

   (3) States can make laws that overturn federal laws.

   (4) The power of each state should depend on how many
   people live in it.

8. Why did the people who wrote the Constitution split the government
   into three branches?

   (1) There was too much for one branch to do.

   (2) Three people wanted to govern the country.

   (3) Each branch could keep the other two from becoming
   too powerful.

   (4) Each section of the country had its own branch.

Check your answers on page 161.

The three branches of government are the legislative, executive, and judicial branches. The writers of the Constitution made sure that the three branches shared power. The Constitution spells out the separate powers for each branch.

Congress is the **legislative branch**. It has the power to make laws. Congress has two sections, or houses. The two houses are called the **Senate** and the **House of Representatives**. States with few people felt that each state should have an equal vote in Congress. However, states with more people felt that they should have more votes. To balance both views, the two houses of Congress are set up differently.

Each state, large or small, elects two members to the Senate. These members are called senators. The Senate has 100 members. Each senator serves for six years. Every two years, one third of the senators must run for re-election. As a result, the membership of the Senate changes slowly.

legislative branch
Congress; it has the power to make laws

Senate
one of the two houses of Congress

House of Representatives
one of the two houses of Congress

The legislative branch passes laws.

In the House of Representatives, the states with more people have more representatives. The House of Representatives has 435 members. The members are elected every two years. Every ten years, the **census** is taken. Based on each new census, the House decides how many representatives each state can have.

Powers of Congress

- makes and changes laws
- collects taxes
- borrows government money
- decides how government money will be spent
- is the only branch that can declare war

The **executive branch** of government carries out the laws. The president is the head of the executive branch of the federal government. The president can also send ideas for new laws to Congress. As commander-in-chief of the armed forces, the president is in charge of defense. The president is elected for a four-year term and may be re-elected only once.

Powers of the President

- appoints people to government jobs
- can direct the fighting during a war
- represents the United States in dealing with other countries

The executive branch also includes fifteen departments that help to run the government. For example, the Treasury Department prints money. The Department of Defense runs the armed forces. The State Department deals with foreign countries. The heads of these fifteen departments make up the president's **cabinet**.

census
an official count of all the people in the country

executive branch
the president and his or her cabinet; this branch makes sure that laws are carried out

cabinet
the group of people who advise the president

The president is head of the executive branch.

GED Tip

Some information on the GED Social Studies Test is shown in charts. Read the title of a chart to find the main idea.

judicial branch
the courts; the branch of government that makes sure laws are constitutional

system of checks and balances
the system that keeps the different branches of government from becoming too powerful

bill
an idea for a law that is presented to Congress

veto
the power of a president to reject a bill

unconstitutional
not following the Constitution

The courts form the **judicial branch** of government. The most powerful, or highest, court is the Supreme Court. There are nine Supreme Court judges, called justices. The president appoints the justices. Then the justices must be approved by the Senate. The justices, once approved, are appointed for life.

Powers of the Supreme Court
- makes sure that federal, state, and local laws follow the Constitution
- explains the meaning of the Constitution
- decides how to apply the Constitution in specific cases

The separation of powers keeps each branch of the government from becoming too powerful. Each branch balances the other two. Each branch keeps the other two under control by limiting what they do. This is called the **system of checks and balances**. An example of this system is when the president sends a **bill** to Congress. Congress can decide not to make the bill a law. On the other hand, the president can refuse to approve a bill that Congress has passed and can **veto** the bill. Finally, the Supreme Court can decide that a law is **unconstitutional**. Congress then has the power to rewrite the law.

The Supreme Court building

Practice

Vocabulary ■ **Write the word that best completes each sentence.**

1. The Congress is made up of two houses called the
   _____ and the House of Representatives.

2. The president has the power to _____
   bills passed by Congress.

3. The courts make up the _____ branch of
   our government.

census

judicial

Senate

veto

Understanding Time Order ■ **Circle the number of the correct answer.**

4. When does the House of Representatives decide how many
   representatives can be sent from each state?

   (1) before the census is taken
   (2) after the census is taken
   (3) while they are working on the census
   (4) every two years when they are elected

5. When do the Supreme Court justices need to be approved
   by Congress?

   (1) before the president appoints them
   (2) after the president appoints them
   (3) after they serve for a year
   (4) when their terms are finished

Comparing and Contrasting ■ **Write your answer.**

6. List two ways that the Senate and the House of Representatives
   are different.

   _____

   _____

   _____

Check your answers on page 161.

GED Skill Strategy

Understanding Cause and Effect

When you study social studies, you need to know the causes and effects of certain events. One thing, a cause, happened. Then another thing, an effect, happened as a result. Words like *because* and *so* show cause and effect. Below are examples of cause and effect.

- *Because* the president vetoed the bill, it did not become a law. The cause is the president vetoing the bill. The effect is the bill did not become a law.
- The senator asked her aide for the papers, *so* the aide left to get them. The cause is the senator asking her aide for the papers. The effect is the aide left to get them.

 Strategy Read the sentences. Ask yourself: Are there clue words for cause and effect?

1. Look for clue words that show cause and effect: *because, reason, so, cause, if, since, as a result, effect, therefore,* and *why.*

2. Use clue words to decide which is the cause and which is the effect.

Exercise 1: Read the paragraph. Underline the key word that helps you see cause and effect.

Some people were afraid that the federal government might have too much power. So the writers of the Constitution split the federal government into three branches.

Exercise 2: Read the sentences below. Write the cause and the effect.

The Constitution was carefully written, so it is still a useful plan of government today.

cause: _____

_____

effect: _____

_____

Part of the Constitution

> **Strategy** Look for key events or ideas. Ask yourself: Did one event or idea cause another?
>
> 1. Identify important events and ideas as you read.
> 2. Decide if events and ideas have a cause-and-effect relationship.
> 3. Pay attention to time order. A cause always happens before its effect.

Exercise 3: Do the following sentences show cause and effect? Write *yes* or *no*.

1. Because no one wanted one branch of the federal government to have too much control, a system of checks and balances was developed. _____

2. No one wanted one branch of the federal government to have too much control. As a result, a system of checks and balances was developed. _____

Exercise 4: Rewrite these sentences to form a paragraph. Use cause-and-effect words.

The court needed a new judge.

The president chose one.

The Senate approved the president's choice.

The judge was appointed to the federal court.

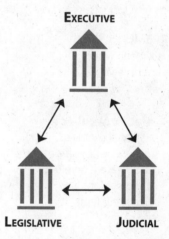

_____

_____

_____

_____

_____

_____

Check your answers on page 162.

Electing the President

candidate
a person who wants
to be elected

political party
a group of people who
share basic positions on
political issues

primary
an election where voters
choose a candidate

convention
a meeting at
which members of a
political party choose
their candidates

poll
a place where
people vote

electoral college
a special group of
representatives from
each state who elect
the president and
vice president

electors
members of the
electoral college

Most presidential **candidates** belong to a **political party**. Many voters belong to a political party, too. There are two main political parties in the United States, the Democratic Party and the Republican Party.

There are two kinds of elections: **primary** and general elections. In a primary, only voters who belong to a political party can vote. They choose a candidate to represent their party. Some states choose candidates with a caucus. In a caucus, members of a political party vote for representatives. The representatives attend meetings to choose the party's candidate. In general elections, voters can choose a candidate from any party.

Presidential elections take place every four years. In the summer before a presidential election, each political party holds a **convention**. Voters from each state send delegates, or representatives, to these conventions. The delegates choose the presidential candidate for their party. They also choose the vice-presidential candidate.

National general elections are held on the first Tuesday in November. Voters go to the **polls** to vote for the president, vice president, and other government positions open that year. In most elections, the winner is the candidate who gets the most votes. However, the president and vice president are elected by the **electoral college**. The electoral college is made up of **electors** from each state and the District of Columbia.

*Citizens voting on
Election Day*

The number of electors from each state depends on how many people live in that state. The electors vote for the candidate who received the most votes in the elector's home state. For example, California has 55 electors. The candidate who gets the most votes in California wins the votes of all 55 of California's electors.

A person can be elected president only twice. This limit of two **terms** is the result of an amendment to the Constitution passed in 1951. Another amendment allows the vice president to act as president if the president dies, resigns, or cannot serve as president.

term
the period of time for which a person holds office

The Right to Vote

For much of U.S. history, there were some adults who were not allowed to vote. In 1788, only free men (not slaves and not women) could vote. Later, women in some states could vote. Gradually, the right to vote was given to more groups of people.

- In 1870, the Fifteenth Amendment to the Constitution was approved. It said that no one could be denied the right to vote because of race.
- In 1920, the Nineteenth Amendment gave women the right to vote in all elections.
- In 1964, the Civil Rights Act made it easier for African Americans to vote.
- In 1971, the Twenty-sixth Amendment gave all citizens aged 18 and older the right to vote.

Still, many Americans do not vote. In the 2004 presidential election, only 60 percent of people who could vote did so.

Before an election, many newspapers print political cartoons. A political cartoon is a drawing that gives an opinion about politics or current events. Political cartoons often use **symbols**.

symbol
picture that stands for something else

Symbol in Cartoon		What It Means
	Globe	The world
	Uncle Sam	The United States
	Bald Eagle	The United States
	White House	The President
	U.S. capitol building	The Congress
	Elephant	The Republican Party
	Donkey	The Democratic Party

GED Tip

You may see a political cartoon on the GED Social Studies Test. Ask yourself: What are the symbols in the cartoon? What do they mean?

In the cartoon, the elephant and the donkey are playing a game. Everything in the cartoon is a symbol:

- The elephant stands for the Republican Party.
- The donkey stands for the Democratic Party.
- The U.S. capitol building stands for Congress.
- The game they are playing looks like Monopoly™. A monopoly is complete control of a business or industry. The game stands for the struggle to control Congress.

This cartoon is about the struggle for power in government. Both political parties want to win the game. They both want to control the government.

Practice

Vocabulary ■ **Write the word or words that best complete each sentence.**

1. Voters from each party choose the _____ for their party in a _____ election.

2. An amendment to the Constitution limits the number of _____ the president can serve.

3. Political cartoons use _____ to stand for things.

candidate

convention

primary

symbols

terms

Understanding Time Order ■ **Circle the number of the correct answer.**

4. Which of the following is the first step in electing a president?

   (1) People vote in a general election.
   (2) People vote in a primary election.
   (3) Political conventions are held.
   (4) The electoral college meets to vote.

5. Which group was last to get the right to vote?

   (1) free men
   (2) women
   (3) African Americans
   (4) adults aged 18 to 20

Understanding Cause and Effect ■ **Circle the number of the correct answer.**

6. Sometimes the number of electors for a particular state changes. What could cause this change?

   (1) the results of a primary election
   (2) a change in the number of Democrats
   (3) a change in the number of Republicans
   (4) a change in the state's population

Check your answers on page 162.

Understanding Political Cartoons

Political cartoons express an opinion, or belief, about an event or issue. Cartoonists draw pictures that are symbols for ideas or things. To understand a political cartoon, you have to look at the picture. Then you have to read the words. Finally, you put the words and pictures together to understand the cartoon's message.

Look at this cartoon. It was printed in a newspaper before an election.

 Strategy   Look at the cartoon. Ask yourself: What is shown in the picture? What do the words mean?

1. Look at the picture. Decide how people or things are used as symbols.

2. Read the words. Sometimes there is a caption, or words written under the picture. Sometimes the words are in "speech balloons." Just like in comic strips, this means that someone is talking.

Exercise 1: Look at the cartoon on page 62. Write your answer to each question below.

1. Who are the people in the cartoon? Who do they represent?

   _____

   _____

2. What are the people in the cartoon talking about?

   _____

   _____

 Strategy   Look at the cartoon again. Ask yourself: What is the topic of this cartoon? What is the cartoonist saying about it?

1. Think about what you already know about the topic of a cartoon. The topic is usually a person or event in the news.

2. Add your own knowledge to the information in the cartoon. Then figure out the cartoon's message.

Exercise 2: Look at the cartoon on page 62 again. Write your answer to each question below.

1. Politicians use negative ads to attack other candidates and their views. Have you ever seen a negative ad on TV?

   _____

2. Why do people complain about negative ads?

   _____

   _____

3. According to the cartoon, why do candidates use negative ads?

   _____

Check your answers on page 162.

civil rights
the basic rights that every citizen is entitled to

segregation
social separation of different groups of people

discriminating
treating groups of people in unequal and unfair ways

Whites and African Americans had to use separate waiting rooms in many states.

The Constitution and the Bill of Rights were written to protect American citizens. Yet when the Constitution was written, many African Americans were slaves. They did not have the **civil rights** that other Americans enjoyed.

It was not until 1865 that the Thirteenth Amendment ended slavery. In 1868, the Fourteenth Amendment declared that all African Americans were citizens. They were entitled to the same protection under the law as any other citizen. Finally, in 1870, the Fifteenth Amendment gave African American men the right to vote.

These new rights were often unfairly applied. Many southern states passed laws allowing **segregation**. African Americans and whites were segregated in public places. These included schools, hotels, train stations, and theaters.

The Civil Rights Act of 1875 was passed to make sure that African Americans were treated equally in public places and on public transportation. In 1883, the Supreme Court said that the federal government could make laws to prevent states from **discriminating** against African Americans. But the Court also said the government could not prevent private citizens and businesses from discriminating.

This court decision slowed down African Americans' struggle for equality. It allowed almost every public place to be segregated. Buses, trains, schools, restaurants, and hospitals were all segregated. Whites and African Americans were separated at work and at play.

Groups fighting for civil rights first formed at the start of the 20th century. At first, little changed, so they took matters into their own hands. They used the First Amendment to fight for their rights.

The First Amendment gives all people the right to speak freely. It also gives all people the right to print their views. The First Amendment protects the people even when they criticize the government.

The First Amendment also protects people's right to form groups. People can hold **demonstrations**. They can sign **petitions**. Demonstrations and petitions are ways to get the government's attention.

In the 1950s and 1960s, Dr. Martin Luther King, Jr., and other leaders organized nonviolent demonstrations and gave speeches asking for more civil rights for African Americans. The government began to pay attention.

demonstration
a public showing of a group's feelings about an issue; for example, a march

petition
a formal request, usually written

In 1957, federal troops were sent to make sure states obeyed laws against segregation.

boycott
to protest a government or any other group by refusing to use or buy its goods

policy
the way an organization is managed; the rules of an organization

disabled
having physical or mental difficulties

ratify
to formally approve

A public school

▶ **GED Tip**

Some passages on the GED Social Studies Test have more than one paragraph. Be sure you understand the main idea of the whole passage.

The process of giving equal rights to all citizens has been a long one. In 1954, the Supreme Court decided the case of *Brown v. the Board of Education of Topeka, Kansas*. In this case, the Supreme Court decided that public education could not be segregated. The court ordered that public schools must stop segregating students. In 1955, in Montgomery, Alabama, African Americans challenged the local laws. They refused to sit in the back of buses. Then they **boycotted** the Montgomery bus system. This forced the bus system to change its **policy**.

In 1964, the Civil Rights Act was passed. The Civil Rights Act protected the voting rights of all citizens. It made segregation illegal and gave the federal government the power to punish anyone who practiced discrimination. The federal government could also cut off money to the states that didn't obey the law.

Over time, other groups began to ask for equal rights. In the 1960s, groups of **disabled** people and those who cared about them began a campaign. In the 1970s, Congress passed laws requiring public schools to accept students with disabilities.

In 1990, Congress passed the Americans with Disabilities Act. This law says that disabled people must be able to use public places, including restaurants, theaters, and stores. There must be parking places for handicapped people and ramps or elevators for people in wheelchairs. Restrooms must be designed for use by a person in a wheelchair. An employer cannot refuse to hire disabled people.

Not all groups working for their civil rights are completely successful, however. The Equal Rights Amendment was passed by Congress in 1972. Its goal was to end discrimination against women. By 1982, it had not been **ratified** by enough states. Therefore, the amendment was not added to the constitution. The Equal Rights Amendment still has not been ratified.

Vocabulary ■ **Write the word that best completes each sentence.**

1. A group was demonstrating for wheelchair ramps at the shopping center. They asked shoppers to sign their _____ .

2. Public schools let in students of all races after the Supreme Court ruled that _____ was not allowed.

3. Many businesses find it a good _____ to help employees get their GED.

petition

policy

segregation

boycott

Cause and Effect ■ **Circle the number of the correct answer.**

4. All African Americans became citizens as a result of

   (1) the Supreme Court decision that reversed the Civil Rights Act of 1875.
   (2) the Fourteenth Amendment to the Constitution.
   (3) the Fifteenth Amendment to the Constitution.
   (4) the African American boycott of the Montgomery bus system.

Comparing and Contrasting ■ **Write the answer to the questions below.**

5. African Americans used both petitions and demonstrations to fight for civil rights.

   (1) How are petitions and demonstrations similar?

   _____

   _____

   (2) How are they different?

   _____

   _____

Check your answers on page 162.

GED Skill Strategy

Recognizing Facts and Opinions

When you read social studies information, you need to know the difference between a fact and an opinion. A fact is something that can be proven to be true. The sentence below is a fact:

- The First Amendment allows freedom of the press.

An opinion is someone's belief or judgment about something. The sentence below is an opinion:

- Newspapers should not print information that could hurt someone.

 Strategy Read the passage. Ask yourself: Are there clue words that show opinions?

1. Look for words that signal opinions: *believe, think, feel,* and *should.*
2. Remember that you can check facts. Beliefs that you may or may not agree with are opinions.

Exercise 1: Read the passage. Underline the clue words that signal opinions.

In the 1950s and 1960s, there were many demonstrations against segregation in the South. Demonstrators protested against "white only" rules. They boycotted a bus company that made African Americans sit in the back of buses. They held sit-ins at restaurants that would not serve African Americans.

Many Americans felt that African Americans were treated unfairly. They believed that civil rights was an important issue. They supported the movement for equality.

Sometimes the police tried to stop the demonstrations. Pictures of police officers beating civil rights workers appeared in newspapers and on television all over the country. These pictures led many more people to believe that African Americans should have equal rights.

▶ **Strategy**   Not all opinions have clue words. When you don't see a clue word in a statement, ask yourself: Is it a fact or is it an opinion?

1. Can you look up the information in the statement? Facts can be looked up and proven. Look for information that you can check.

2. Is the statement an opinion? Opinions cannot be proven. You may agree with them, or you may disagree.

Exercise 2: Put an *F* for fact or an *O* for opinion next to each statement.

_____ **1.** People opposed slavery in the 1800s.

_____ **2.** I think slavery is wrong.

_____ **3.** The Nineteenth Amendment gives women the right to vote.

_____ **4.** The Nineteenth Amendment is the most important Amendment.

_____ **5.** Women and men should have equal rights.

_____ **6.** Several women organized a women's rights convention in 1848.

Exercise 3: Look at pages 64–66. Write two facts from these pages. Add an opinion of your own about the facts you have chosen.

Fact 1: _____

Fact 2: _____

Opinion: _____

_____

In 1963, more than 200,000 Americans joined a civil rights march on Washington.

Check your answers on page 163.

Previewing Passages

On the GED Social Studies Test, you will read passages and then answer questions. One way to understand a passage is to preview it first. Read the first sentence. The first sentence often tells the main idea. Then skim the rest of the passage. That way, you can figure out the topic and main idea. Finally, go back and carefully read the entire passage.

 Strategy   Try the strategy on the example below. Use these steps.

Step 1   Read the first sentence. Think about what it says.

Step 2   Skim the rest of the passage. Look for the main idea.

Step 3   Read the passage carefully. Take your time.

Step 4   Answer the questions.

In the United States, power is divided between the federal government and the state governments. The federal government has certain powers. For example, it makes coins and prints money. The states have other powers. For example, the states control how elections are held. Some powers are held by both federal and state governments. For example, both can collect taxes.

What is the topic of the paragraph?

(1) the powers of the government

(2) the division of power between federal and state governments

(3) the powers of state governments

(4) the powers to collect taxes from U.S. citizens

In Step 1 you read the first sentence. It says that power is divided between the federal and state governments. In Step 2 you skimmed the paragraph, looking for the main idea. In Step 3 you read the paragraph carefully. In Step 4 you answered the question. The correct answer is (2). The topic of the paragraph is the division of power between the federal government and the states. Choices (1), (3), and (4) are details that do not completely describe the topic.

Practice

Practice the strategy. Use the steps you learned. Circle the number of the correct answer.

The Sixth Amendment lists the rights of people accused of committing crimes. Accused people have the right to a speedy trial by jury. They have the right to know what crimes they are accused of. They also have the right to a lawyer who can help with their defense.

1. What is the main idea of this paragraph?

   (1) People have the right to know what crimes they are accused of.

   (2) People accused of crimes have the right to a lawyer.

   (3) People accused of crimes have the right to a speedy trial.

   (4) People accused of crimes have Sixth Amendment rights.

Practice the strategy. Use the steps you learned. Circle the number of the correct answer.

All states have a legislature that makes state laws. In most states, the legislature has two parts: a senate and a house. Only Nebraska has a legislature with just one part.

The members of most state legislatures serve part-time. They also have other jobs. To some legislators, serving in the state legislature is just the beginning of their political careers. Their goal may be to run for governor or for Congress.

2. What would be a good title for this passage?

   (1) Nebraska's One-House Legislature

   (2) From the State Legislature to the Governor's House

   (3) Overview of State Legislatures

   (4) The Three Branches of State Government

3. Why can most members of state legislatures have other jobs?

   (1) They want to become governor.

   (2) They serve only part-time in the legislature.

   (3) They want to become members of Congress.

   (4) They want to live like ordinary Americans.

Check your answers on page 163.

Read each selection and question carefully. Circle the number of the correct answer.

<u>**Questions 1–3 are based on the following passage.**</u>

> What happens if two candidates get the same number of votes in a national election? If there is a tie for president in the electoral college, then Congress must vote. The House of Representatives elects the president. The Senate elects the vice president.
>
> States also have to deal with tie votes. Montana had a tie vote in one election. In that case, the state legislature voted to break the tie. Wyoming also had a tie vote in an election. Election workers wrote the candidates' names on two Ping-Pong™ balls. They put the balls in the governor's hat. An election worker then picked one of the balls. The candidate with his name on the ball was the winner. Some voters thought that was not a good way to choose the winner.

1. What would be the result of a tie vote in the electoral college?
   (1) State legislatures would choose the president.
   (2) The vice president would break the tie.
   (3) Congress would vote for the president and vice president.
   (4) The two candidates would pick names to see who wins.

2. Why did the Montana legislature have to decide an election?
   (1) Both candidates were from the same political party.
   (2) Both candidates got the same number of votes.
   (3) Only legislators may vote in Montana.
   (4) Only legislators may count the votes.

3. Which of the following is an opinion?
   (1) Sometimes an election ends in a tie.
   (2) Normally, the electoral college elects the president.
   (3) There are different ways to deal with tie votes.
   (4) Pulling a name from a hat is a poor way to break a tie vote.

Questions 4–6 are based on the following cartoon.

4. What does the cartoon show?

   (1) one man trying to get another man to vote

   (2) two election workers talking about voting

   (3) instructions on how to vote

   (4) two men talking about a candidate

5. Who is the short man a symbol of?

   (1) a Democratic candidate

   (2) a Republican candidate

   (3) a voter

   (4) an election worker

6. Which of the following is the cartoonist's opinion?

   (1) Voters can vote by mail.

   (2) Voters can vote at "early voting" places.

   (3) Voters don't care enough to vote.

   (4) Voters can get rides to the polls.

The men who wrote the Constitution set a four-year term for the president. The first president, George Washington, served only two terms. Over the next 150 years, presidents followed his example. Two terms became the traditional limit.

During the Great Depression and World War II, Franklin D. Roosevelt was elected president four times. Many people thought four terms was too many. In 1951, the Constitution was amended. The Twenty-second Amendment limited a president to two terms.

7. What caused the two-term limit to become a tradition?

    (1) the four-year term set by the Constitution

    (2) Washington's serving only two terms as president

    (3) the election of Franklin D. Roosevelt

    (4) the Twenty-second Amendment to the Constitution

8. Which of the following is an opinion rather than a fact?

    (1) The president serves a four-year term.

    (2) Originally, there were no term limits on the presidency.

    (3) An amendment put a two-term limit on the presidency.

    (4) Four terms is too many terms for a president to serve.

Check your answers on page 163.

Unit 2 Skill Check-Up Chart

Check your answers. In the first column, circle the numbers of any questions you missed. Then look across the rows to see the skills you need to review and the pages where you can find each skill.

Question	Skill	Page
1, 2, 7	Understanding Cause and Effect	56–57
3, 8	Recognizing Facts and Opinions	68–69
4, 5, 6	Understanding Political Cartoons	62–63

Unit 3   Geography

continent

equator

monsoon

climate

In this unit, you will learn about

- maps and what they show
- North and South America
- Europe and Africa
- Asia, Australia, and Antarctica

Geography is the study of our planet's places. Much geography information can be found on maps.

Write about a time you used a map.

_____

_____

When you study geography, you learn about continents and countries. You learn about the land and how people use it.

Name two countries.

_____

_____

One way to learn about the world is to study maps. There are many kinds of maps. Each kind of map shows different information. Maps can show all or part of the earth's surface. For example, a world map shows the whole world. A globe is a round map that shows the whole world. A political map shows countries. A road map shows different routes from one place to another.

The map on page 77 is a world map. Looking at this map, you see that the earth's surface is mostly water. Almost three fourths of the earth is covered by oceans. There are four main oceans: the Pacific Ocean, the Atlantic Ocean, the Indian Ocean, and the Arctic Ocean.

continent
one of the seven large areas of land on the earth

The map also shows major land areas, called **continents**. The two halves, or sides, of the earth are called **hemispheres**. The continents of North and South America are in the Western Hemisphere. The continents of Europe, Asia, Africa, and Australia are in the Eastern Hemisphere.

hemisphere
half of the world;
hemi- means "half"; a sphere is a ball or a globe

Maps use lines to help you find places. The map on page 77 shows the **equator**, an imaginary line that circles the earth. It cuts the earth into a northern half and a southern half. The northern half is the Northern Hemisphere. The southern half is the Southern Hemisphere.

equator
an imaginary line around the middle of the earth

key
the part of a map that shows what the different lines and symbols mean

Most maps have a **key**. Look at the key in the bottom right corner of the map on page 77. The key gives information you need to read the map. It explains any lines, markings, and symbols. This key tells you that dashed lines show divisions between continents.

compass rose
the symbol on a map that shows the four directions: north, east, south, and west

Most maps also have a **compass rose**. The compass rose shows you directions on the map. Look at the compass rose in the top left corner of the map on page 77. It shows the directions north (N), east (E), south (S), and west (W).

The Continents of the World

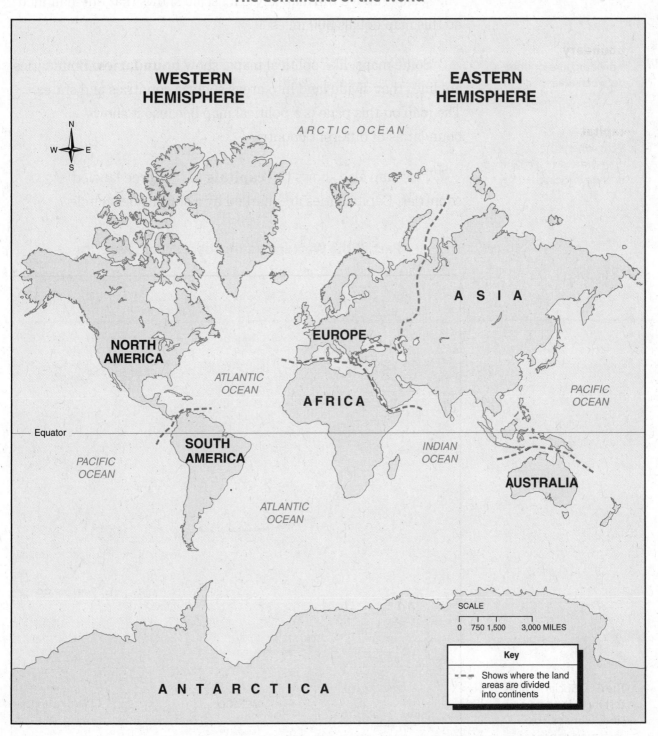

scale
a line that helps the reader measure distances on the map

boundary
a dividing line, or border, between areas

capital
a city where the government of a country or state is located

Most maps have a **scale**. A map's scale helps you measure the distance from one place to another. Look at the map on this page. The scale is above the map key. The scale shows that one-half inch on this map equals 500 miles.

Some maps, like political maps, show **boundaries**. Boundaries are lines that divide land into areas such as countries and states. The map on this page is a political map because it shows boundaries of different countries.

This map also shows the **capitals** of the three labeled countries. Capital cities are marked by a star inside a circle.

Part of the Western Hemisphere: North America

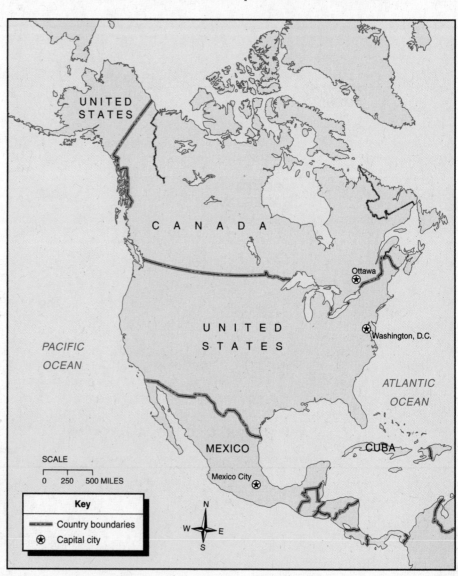

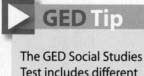

GED Tip

The GED Social Studies Test includes different kinds of maps. For each map, check the key. This will help you understand details shown on the map.

Practice

Vocabulary ■ Write the word that best completes each sentence.

1. A _____ gives you information you need to read a map.

2. The land areas of the earth are divided into seven _____ .

3. The dashed lines between Europe and Asia on the map on page 77 show the _____ between the two continents.

boundary

continents

hemisphere

key

Finding Facts ■ Circle the number of the correct answer.

4. Which covers the largest area?

   (1) the oceans

   (2) Asia

   (3) Australia

   (4) North America

5. Which statement is true?

   (1) The earth's surface is covered mostly by land.

   (2) The earth's land is divided into continents.

   (3) A globe is a map that shows three fourths of the earth.

   (4) There are nine continents.

Recognizing Fact and Opinion ■ Circle the number of the correct answer.

6. Which of the following is an opinion?

   (1) The map scale shows distance on a map.

   (2) Boundaries divide areas from each other.

   (3) The best type of map is a road map.

   (4) A globe shows the earth as a sphere.

Check your answers on page 164.

Reading Maps

Learning to read maps is important. The map key explains map symbols and shaded areas. A map often has a scale. The scale can help you measure distances.

▶ **Strategy** Look at the map. Ask yourself: How can I use the scale to find distance?

1. Lay a piece of paper across the distance you want to measure. Put two large marks on the paper to show the points at each end of the distance.

2. Hold your paper against the scale. Line up the first mark with the zero on the scale. Then put a small mark on the paper to show where the scale ends.

3. The distance you marked may be longer than the scale. If so, line the small mark up with the zero on the scale. Make another small mark where the scale ends. Continue marking until you have counted out the entire distance between the two large marks.

4. Count the number of times the scale fits into the distance you are measuring. Multiply this amount by the number of miles represented by the scale. This is the total in miles for the distance you are measuring.

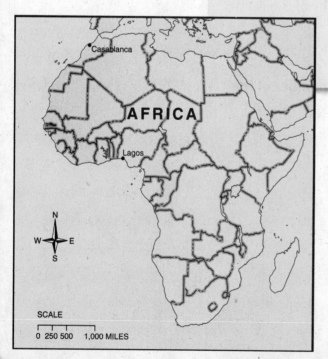

Exercise 1: Look at the map of Africa. Use a piece of paper and the map scale to find distances. Complete the sentences.

1. The distance across the widest part of Africa is about _____ miles.

2. The distance from Casablanca to Lagos is about _____ miles.

Strategy Look at the map. Ask yourself: What kind of details are on this map?

1. Look at the key for this map. See what each line, symbol, and pattern shows.

2. Locate an area on the map. Match the lines, symbols, and patterns there to the ones on the key to learn details about the area you chose.

Exercise 2: Look at the map of Australia. Answer the questions about its climate.

1. What are the three types of climate found in Australia?

_____

2. Which climate affects the largest area?

_____

3. Where is Australia's climate wet?

(1) in the center

(2) along the northern coast

(3) along the southern coast

(4) along the northern and southern coasts

Australia's Climate

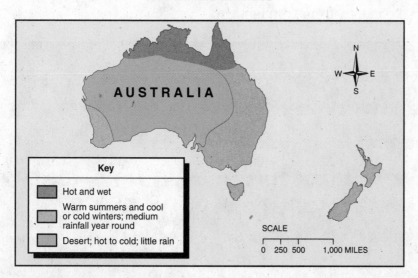

Check your answers on page 164.

North and South America

Central America
the countries between Mexico and South America

plain
a large area of flat land

climate
the average weather conditions in a particular place

export
to sell and send goods to other countries

mineral
a solid substance, like iron or salt, found in the earth

tourism
the business of providing services for people who are traveling for pleasure

North America. There are three large countries in North America: Canada, the United States, and Mexico. North America also includes seven small countries, located in **Central America**. There are also many island countries in the Caribbean Sea.

North America has high mountains in the west. These are the Rocky Mountains. There are lower mountains in the east. These are the Appalachian Mountains. Between the Rocky Mountains and the Appalachian Mountains are wide, flat **plains** called the Great Plains.

In the far north, the **climate** is cold all year round. In the far south, it is hot all year round. In most of North America, summer is hot and winter is cold.

The United States and Canada have a lot of good farmland and get enough rain to raise crops. Both countries grow more food than they need. They **export** extra food, sending it to other countries. North America is also rich in oil, coal, and other **minerals**. Canada, the United States, and Mexico also make and export many different manufactured goods.

Mexico and the Caribbean islands have beautiful beaches. Many people visit these countries on vacation. These countries make money from **tourism**.

The Great Plains of North America

North and South America

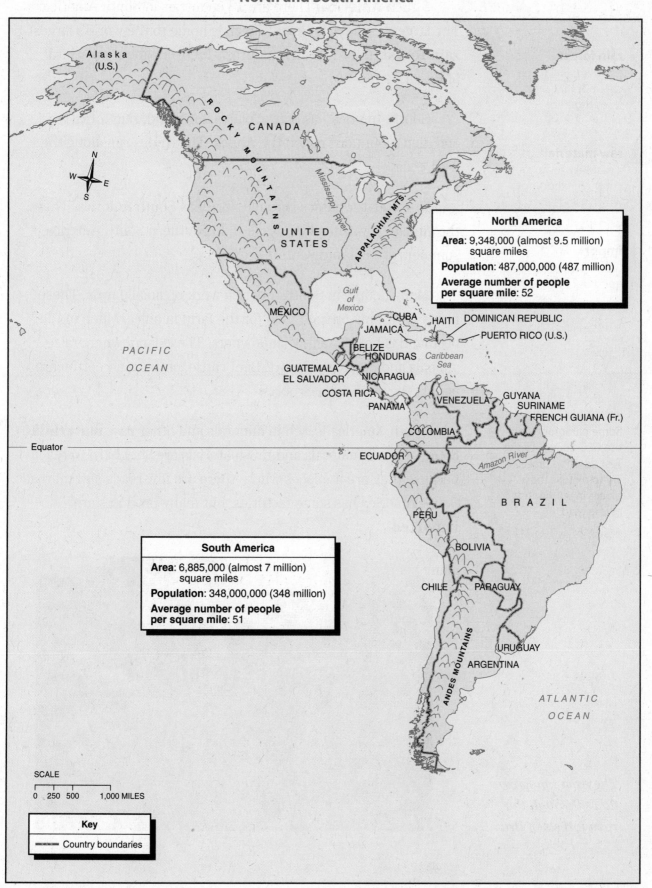

North America

Area: 9,348,000 (almost 9.5 million) square miles

Population: 487,000,000 (487 million)

Average number of people per square mile: 52

South America

Area: 6,885,000 (almost 7 million) square miles

Population: 348,000,000 (348 million)

Average number of people per square mile: 51

Alaska (U.S.)

CANADA

ROCKY MOUNTAINS

Mississippi River

UNITED STATES

APPALACHIAN MTS.

Gulf of Mexico

MEXICO

CUBA

JAMAICA

HAITI

DOMINICAN REPUBLIC

PUERTO RICO (U.S.)

BELIZE

HONDURAS

Caribbean Sea

GUATEMALA

EL SALVADOR

NICARAGUA

COSTA RICA

PANAMA

VENEZUELA

GUYANA

SURINAME

FRENCH GUIANA (Fr.)

COLOMBIA

ECUADOR

Amazon River

BRAZIL

PERU

BOLIVIA

CHILE

PARAGUAY

ANDES MOUNTAINS

URUGUAY

ARGENTINA

PACIFIC OCEAN

Equator

ATLANTIC OCEAN

SCALE

0   250 500   1,000 MILES

Key

- - - - Country boundaries

rain forest
a wet tropical forest with tall trees that grow very close together

raw material
a natural substance, like cotton or wood, from which goods are made

import
to buy and bring foreign goods into a country

GED Tip

Some paragraphs on the GED Social Studies Test describe places. Try to picture these places in your mind as you read.

South America. There are 13 countries in South America. The largest country is Brazil. Brazil is home to the world's largest **rain forest**, the Amazon rain forest. It covers about one third of Brazil.

South America has grassy plains, farmland, rain forests, and high mountains called the Andes. The Andes run along the west coast.

The equator passes through northern South America. There, the climate is warm all year round. In southern South America, summers are hot and winters are cold.

Many people in South America work on small farms. These farms grow only enough food for the farm families. Much of the best land is held by a few landowners. These landowners raise animals and crops for export. Beef cattle, coffee, and cotton are among the main farm exports.

South America is rich in minerals and other **raw materials**. Some of these minerals and raw materials are very hard to reach because they are in places where there are few roads and railroads. South America has some factories, but many products are **imported**.

The Amazon River flows through the rain forests of Brazil.

Practice

Vocabulary ■ Write the word that best completes each sentence.

1. The United States and Canada grow enough food
   to _____ to other countries.

2. Between the mountain ranges in North America are large,
   flat areas called _____.

3. The _____ is the average weather conditions of
   a place.

export

climate

import

plains

Reading a Map ■ Look at the map on page 83. Write your answers.

4. Which two countries in South America are farthest south?

   _____

5. Which river flows into the Gulf of Mexico?

   _____

6. Which seven countries are located in Central America?

   _____

   _____

7. Which ocean is west of North and South America?

   _____

**Comparing and Contrasting ■ Write your answer to the
question below.**

8. How are the United States and Canada alike in terms of farming and
   manufacturing?

   _____

   _____

   _____

   _____

Check your answers on page 164.

Europe. Europe is not much larger than the United States. However, more than twice as many people live in Europe. Most of the 48 countries of Europe are very small. Many of them are world powers. France, Germany, and the United Kingdom are countries in Europe. Part of Russia is also in Europe.

Almost all of Europe is near the sea. Europe has a long, jagged coastline with many good harbors for ships. There are mountains in the north and the south.

Europe is quite far north. However, its winters are usually fairly mild. Norway, Sweden, and Finland, which are partly in the **Arctic**, have warmer winters than the Canadian arctic because of a warm ocean current called the Gulf Stream. The Gulf Stream carries warm water from the Gulf of Mexico to Europe. Winds blowing from this warm water keep temperatures in Europe mild. Find the Gulf Stream on the map below.

Arctic
area surrounding the North Pole and including some of northern Europe, North America, and Asia

industrialized
an area with many factories

natural resources
things found in nature, such as land, water, forests, and minerals

The Gulf Stream

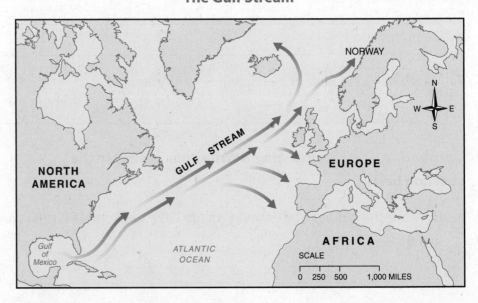

Europe is an **industrialized** continent. It has modern mining, manufacturing, and farming. Europe has **natural resources** like coal and iron. It also has rich soil and good rainfall for crops. Over half the land is used for farming. Europe produces enough food to feed its large population.

Europe and Africa

ICELAND

NORWAY **SWEDEN** **FINLAND**

R U S S I A

ESTONIA

UNITED KINGDOM **DENMARK** LATVIA

LITHUANIA

IRELAND NETHERLANDS RUSSIA **BELARUS**

BELGIUM

GERMANY **POLAND**

N

W E LUXEMBOURG CZECH **UKRAINE**
REPUBLIC SLOVAKIA
S LIECHTENSTEIN
AUSTRIA HUNGARY MOLDOVA
SWITZERLAND
SLOVENIA ROMANIA
FRANCE CROATIA
BOS. & SERBIA
HERZG. AND MONTENEGRO

ATLANTIC BULGARIA **GEORGIA**
OCEAN ANDORRA **ITALY** MACEDONIA
ALBANIA **TURKEY** **ARMENIA**
SPAIN GREECE
PORTUGAL AZERBAIJAN

MALTA A S I A

TUNISIA Mediterranean Sea

MOROCCO

ALGERIA

LIBYA

WESTERN **EGYPT**
SAHARA
(MOR.) S A H A R A   D E S E R T

MAURITANIA
A F R I C A

MALI **NIGER**
CAPE
VERDE ERITREA
SENEGAL **CHAD** DJIBOUTI
GAMBIA **SUDAN**
BURKINA
GUINEA- FASO **ETHIOPIA** SOMALIA
BISSAU GUINEA
NIGERIA
SIERRA LEONE COTE
D'IVOIRE CENTRAL AFRICAN
LIBERIA GHANA REPUBLIC
BENIN **CAMEROON**
TOGO UGANDA
EQUATORIAL **KENYA**
GUINEA CONGO

GABON RWANDA **INDIAN**
Equator BURUNDI **OCEAN**
DEMOCRATIC
REPUBLIC OF
THE CONGO TANZANIA

COMOROS
ANGOLA MALAWI

ZAMBIA

ZIMBABWE **MADAGASCAR**
ATLANTIC
OCEAN NAMIBIA MOZAMBIQUE

BOTSWANA

SWAZILAND

SOUTH
AFRICA LESOTHO

Nile River

Europe

Area: 4,063,000 (4 million) square miles

Population: 730,000,000 (730 million)

Average number of people per square mile: 180

Africa

Area: 11,707,000 (almost 12 million) square miles

Population: 803,000,000 (803 million)

Average number of people per square mile: 69

SCALE

0   250   500   1,000 MILES

Key

- - - Country boundaries

Africa. Africa is a large continent. It contains over 50 countries, including Egypt, Ethiopia, Nigeria, and South Africa. The world's longest river, the Nile, is in Africa. Africa also has the world's largest desert, the Sahara. More than two fifths of Africa is desert. Another two fifths is **grassland**. Rain forests cover a little less than one fifth of the land.

The equator passes through Africa. As a result, the climate of most of Africa is warm or hot all year. Rainfall varies widely. For example, the deserts get less than ten inches of rain a year. However, some places along the coast get 150 inches of rain a year.

Africa has some large cities, such as Cairo and Lagos. However, many people in Africa live in small villages. There they tend animals or farm. Some places lack good soil. Others don't get enough rain. As a result, farming is very difficult.

Africa is rich in minerals. Northern Africa has rich oil resources. Most of the world's gold and fine diamonds come from Africa. Africa also has other rare minerals. Many African countries are developing their mineral resources. They sell oil and minerals to industrialized nations.

grassland
a large area of grass such as a plain

Cairo is one of the largest cities in Africa. It is the capital of Egypt.

> ▶ **GED Tip**
>
> When taking the GED Social Studies Test, remember that the topic sentence of a paragraph tells the main idea. Finding the main idea will help you to understand the paragraph.

Practice

Vocabulary ■ Write the word that best completes each sentence.

1. About two fifths of Africa's land is _____ , which provides food for grazing animals.

2. Europe is an _____ continent; it has many factories.

3. The _____ is the area around the North Pole.

> Arctic
>
> grassland
>
> industrialized
>
> resources

Reading a Map ■ Look at the map of some countries in Africa. Write your answers.

East Africa

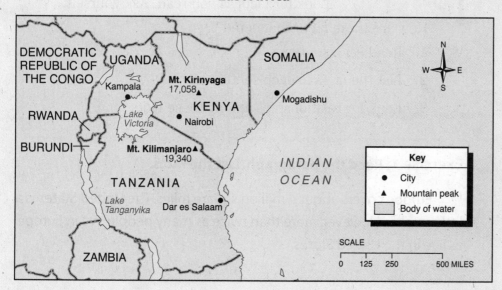

4. Which three countries border Lake Victoria?

_____

5. Which country has the highest mountain?

_____

Comparing and Contrasting ■ Write your answer to the question below.

6. How does farming in Africa differ from farming in Europe?

_____

_____

_____

Check your answers on page 165.

GED Skill Strategy

Making Inferences

When you read, you can get more information than is stated. This process is called making inferences. You make inferences by putting together facts and ideas from what you read. You combine these with what you already know. For example, you read that Europe produces many manufactured goods. You already know that such goods are made in factories. From these facts, you can infer that Europe has many factories.

 Strategy Look for facts as you read. Ask yourself: How are these facts connected?

1. Read each sentence.
2. List the facts in each sentence.
3. Look for relationships among these facts.

Exercise 1: Read the paragraph. List the facts.

Europe covers about 4 million square miles. The United States is a little smaller. However, more than twice as many people live in Europe as live in the United States.

_____

_____

Exercise 2: Read the paragraph in Exercise 1 again. Then choose the best inference. Circle the number of the correct answer.

What can you infer about Europe and the United States?

(1) There are more people per square mile in Europe than in the United States.

(2) There are fewer people per square mile in Europe than in the United States.

(3) There are about the same number of people per square mile in Europe and the United States.

Many people in Europe live in cities.

> **Strategy** As you read, think about the facts in a passage. Ask yourself: What do I already know about the subject?
>
> **1.** Look for information in the passage.
>
> **2.** Think about what you already know about this information.
>
> **3.** Combine the new information with what you already know.

Exercise 3: Read the sentences. List some facts you already know about deserts. Then write what you already know about conditions needed for farming.

     Africa has the world's largest desert, the Sahara. More than two fifths of Africa is desert.

_____

_____

_____

Exercise 4: Add the facts in the sentences above to what you already know. Choose the best inference. Circle the number of the correct answer.

What can you infer about farming in Africa?

(1) Farms cover all of Africa.

(2) Floods are a problem in all of Africa.

(3) Large parts of Africa cannot be farmed.

(4) There is not enough water to farm in Africa.

Exercise 5: List one fact from the sentences that supports your inference.

_____

_____

Check your answers on page 165.

Asia. The largest continent is Asia. It contains one third of all the land in the world. Asia is so big that different parts have very different climates. The far north of Asia is very cold. The south, southwest, and southeast are very hot. More than half of the world's population lives in Asia.

Southwest Asia includes Saudi Arabia, Iran, Iraq, Israel, and a number of other countries. This part of Asia is also called the Middle East. Much of this area is rich in oil.

In some parts of Southwest Asia, the temperature can reach 115°F during the day. As in other areas of the world, some of the people farm. Others live and work in cities. A few are nomads, or people who move from place to place with their animals. There are about 114 people per square mile in Southwest Asia.

South Asia consists largely of India, Pakistan, Bangladesh, and Sri Lanka. The world's tallest mountains, the Himalayas, are found there. South Asia has good farmland. However, there are many people to feed, as there are 877 people per square mile.

Southeast Asia includes Vietnam, Thailand, Indonesia, and the Philippines. This part of Asia is rich in natural resources. It has forests, good farmland, water, and minerals.

monsoon
wind in southern Asia; it brings heavy rains to this area each year

In southern parts of Asia, there are seasonal winds. They are called **monsoons**. For part of the year, the winds blow from the land toward the ocean. These winds are dry. Then the winds change direction. They blow from the ocean over the land. These winds bring heavy rains.

East Asia includes China, North Korea, South Korea, and Japan. There are about 337 people per square mile in East Asia. Many live in large industrial cities such as Yokohama and Shanghai.

Asia and Australia

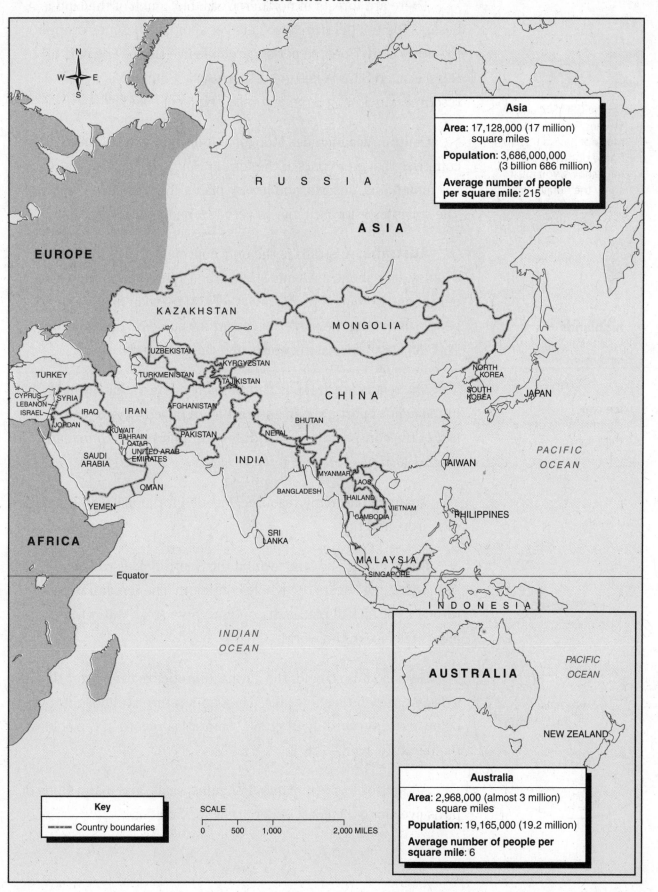

Asia

Area: 17,128,000 (17 million) square miles

Population: 3,686,000,000 (3 billion 686 million)

Average number of people per square mile: 215

RUSSIA

ASIA

EUROPE

KAZAKHSTAN

MONGOLIA

UZBEKISTAN

KYRGYZSTAN

TURKEY

TURKMENISTAN

TAJIKISTAN

NORTH KOREA

CYPRUS
LEBANON
ISRAEL

SYRIA

IRAQ

IRAN

AFGHANISTAN

CHINA

SOUTH KOREA

JAPAN

JORDAN

BHUTAN

KUWAIT
BAHRAIN
QATAR
UNITED ARAB
EMIRATES

PAKISTAN

NEPAL

TAIWAN

PACIFIC OCEAN

SAUDI ARABIA

INDIA

MYANMAR

LAOS

OMAN

BANGLADESH

THAILAND

VIETNAM

YEMEN

CAMBODIA

PHILIPPINES

AFRICA

SRI LANKA

Equator

MALAYSIA

SINGAPORE

INDONESIA

INDIAN OCEAN

AUSTRALIA

PACIFIC OCEAN

NEW ZEALAND

Australia

Area: 2,968,000 (almost 3 million) square miles

Population: 19,165,000 (19.2 million)

Average number of people per square mile: 6

Key

— Country boundaries

SCALE

0   500   1,000   2,000 MILES

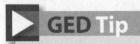
GED Tip

On the GED Social Studies Test, a map may not have a title. To figure out what the map shows, you must study the details.

There are forests in northern Asia, but much of the land is desert. The temperature also gets very cold, sometimes dropping to −40°F. Only 7 people per square mile live there. The part of Russia called Siberia lies in northern Asia. Siberia has many resources, including large amounts of oil, coal, and iron.

Central Asia includes Mongolia. It also includes some countries that were part of the former Soviet Union. Central Asia has mountains, deserts, and grassy plains. The climate is very dry. The soil is poor for farming, so very few people live there.

Australia. Australia is the only continent that is also a country. It is about the same size as the United States. However, only about 19 million people live there. More than half of the people live along the eastern coast or in the nearby **highlands**. The climate in the east is warm, and the farmland is rich.

The rest of Australia is flat. In many areas, rainfall is light. In the central parts, sheep and cattle are raised. The western half of the continent is mostly desert. Temperatures there can reach 120°F.

Australia has many resources needed for industry. It is rich in coal, iron, and tin.

Antarctica. The land around the South Pole is called Antarctica. Ice covers the whole continent. The **ice cap** is nearly three miles thick in places. It contains more fresh water than anywhere else in the world.

Because it is so cold, the air in Antarctica is even drier than in a desert. Very little snow falls. The temperature is almost always below freezing. On July 21, 1983, Antarctica recorded the coldest temperature ever, −128°F.

Antarctica has few plants. Penguins, seals, and many kinds of birds live along the coast, where they feed on fish.

highlands
land that is higher than land near the ocean

ice cap
a permanent cover of thick ice

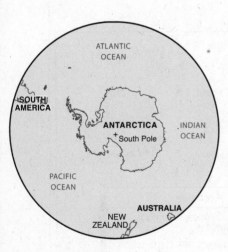

Practice

Vocabulary ■ **Write the word or words that best complete each sentence.**

1. Each year, the _____ brings heavy rain to southern Asia.

2. In some areas of Antarctica, the _____ is almost three miles thick.

ice cap

monsoon

highlands

Reading a Map ■ **Look at the map on page 94. Write your answers.**

3. Which oceans surround Antarctica?

_____

4. What important point is found in Antarctica?

_____

Making Inferences ■ **Circle the number of the correct answer.**

5. Asia is so big that different parts have very different climates. People in different parts of Asia probably

   (1) eat one type of food.
   (2) raise similar crops.
   (3) build the same type of home.
   (4) dress in different types of clothing.

6. More than half of the people in Australia live along the eastern coast or in the nearby highlands. The central and western parts of the country are probably

   (1) not very populated.
   (2) crowded and noisy.
   (3) filled with shopping malls.
   (4) important centers of business.

Check your answers on page 165.

Previewing Graphics

Graphics include charts, tables, and diagrams. One way to read a graphic is to preview it. Previewing involves looking over the graphic to see what it is about. Reading the title is the first step. The title often tells the topic. Next, read the column heads of a chart or a table, or skim the labels of a diagram. This can help you figure out the main idea. Knowing the topic and main idea make understanding the graphic easier. Finally, look at the graphic closely, and study the details.

 Strategy   Try the strategy on the example below. Use these steps.

Step 1 Read the title. What is the topic of the graphic?

Step 2 Read the column heads, or labels. What do they show?

Step 3 Look at the graphic carefully. Take your time.

Step 4 Answer the question.

Example

Largest Metropolitan Areas in the World (Year 2000)

Rank	City	Population
1	Tokyo, Japan	27,900,000
2	Mumbai, India	18,100,000
3	São Paulo, Brazil	17,800,000

What does this table show?

(1) the world's three most important cities

(2) the population of the world's three largest cities

(3) population growth in the world's largest cities

(4) the population of the largest cities in the United States

In Step 1 you read the title. The topic of the table is the world's largest cities. In Step 2 you read the column heads. The cities are ranked by population. In Step 3 you read the whole table carefully. In Step 4 you answered the question. The correct answer is (2). The table shows the population of the world's three largest cities.

Practice the strategy. Use the steps you learned. Circle the number of the correct answer.

Three Ways to Show Elevation (Heights) on Maps

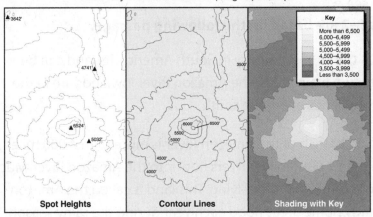

| Spot Heights | Contour Lines | Shading with Key |

1. What is the main idea of this diagram?

   (1) Map keys show elevation.

   (2) Labels are the best way to show elevation.

   (3) Elevation can be shown in different ways on maps.

   (4) Elevation refers to the height of land.

Practice the strategy. Use the steps you learned. Circle the number of the correct answer.

Two Nations on the Island of Hispaniola

	Dominican Republic	Haiti
Population	8,950,034	8,121,622
Main religion	Roman Catholic (95%)	Roman Catholic (80%)
Languages	Spanish	French, Creole
Main occupation	Services and government	Farming

2. What does this chart show?

   (1) natural resources of the Dominican Republic and Haiti

   (2) political systems of the Dominican Republic and Haiti

   (3) physical features of the island of Hispaniola

   (4) facts about the people of the Dominican Republic and Haiti

Check your answers on page 165.

Read each passage and question carefully. Circle the number of the correct answer.

Questions 1–2 are based on the following passage.

Brazil is the largest country in South America. Its land can be divided into two main areas. The Amazon River lowlands are in the north. The highlands are in the south.

The main branch of the Amazon River is more than 4,000 miles long. More than 1,000 smaller rivers flow into the Amazon River. Much of the surrounding land is low-lying. This land is called the Amazon River lowlands. Some areas flood each year during the rainy season. The climate is warm year-round. Rain forests thrive there.

The highlands cover southern Brazil. The land is raised and fairly flat. It is a plateau. Deep river valleys cut through the plateau. The climate in the highlands is cooler and less rainy than in the Amazon lowlands.

1. Why are the southern highlands likely to have good conditions for farming?
   (1) The climate is very warm.
   (2) The climate is rainy and the land is low-lying.
   (3) The land has deep valleys.
   (4) The land is high and flat and less likely to flood.

2. What is likely to be the best way to transport goods in the Amazon lowlands?
   (1) by truck
   (2) by train
   (3) by boat
   (4) by foot

Questions 3–5 are based on the following map.

Europe and Asia: Climate

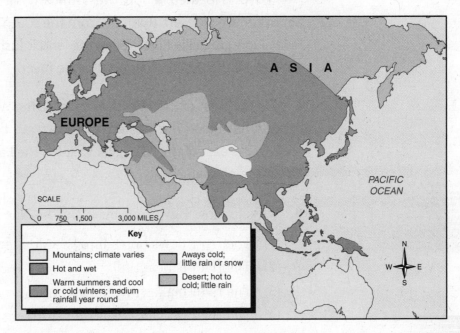

3. What does the map show?

   (1) the climate in the Western Hemisphere

   (2) the climate in Europe and Asia

   (3) political boundaries in Europe and Asia

   (4) landforms in Europe and Asia

4. Which region shown on the map has desert conditions?

   (1) western Europe

   (2) the mountains of South Asia

   (3) southwest Asia

   (4) southeast Asia

5. Which clothing would be best to wear in northern Asia?

   (1) clothing that keeps you warm

   (2) clothing that keeps the rain off

   (3) clothing that keeps you cool

   (4) clothing that doesn't show dust

Questions 6–7 are based on the following passage.

Egypt is located in northwest Africa. It is a sandy plateau and almost entirely desert. Running from the south to the north is the Nile River. Along the Nile River Valley, the land is lush and green. Almost all the people of Egypt live along the Nile River.

To the west of the Nile River Valley is the Western Desert, which is a rocky, sandy place. The Western Desert covers two thirds of Egypt's land area. To the east of the Nile River Valley is the Eastern Desert. It is a dry limestone plateau.

6. Why do most Egyptians live near the Nile River?

    (1) The river flows north into the Mediterranean Sea.

    (2) The river is beautiful.

    (3) The river makes the climate rainy.

    (4) The river provides water for drinking and farming.

7. What can you infer about the Western Desert?

    (1) People there grow many crops for export.

    (2) The area has more water than the Nile River Valley.

    (3) Very few people live there.

    (4) The climate is good for large-scale farming.

Check your answers on page 166.

Unit 3 Skill Check-Up Chart

Check your answers. In the first column, circle the numbers of any questions that you missed. Then look across the rows to see the skills you need to review and the pages where you can find each skill.

Question	Skill	Pages
1, 2, 5, 6, 7	Making Inferences	90–91
3, 4	Reading Maps	80–81

Unit 4 World History

empire

imperialism

civilization

knight

In this unit, you will learn about

- civilizations of the ancient world
- the Middle Ages and the Renaissance
- the Industrial Revolution and imperialism
- the world wars and global changes of the twentieth century

World history is the study of past events from all over the globe. World history is important because past events affect us here and now.

List one important historical event that has happened in your lifetime.

_____

_____

When you study world history, you learn about people and societies all over the world. You learn about important changes that took place.

List one important historical event that happened before you were born.

_____

_____

civilization
a large, complex society with cities, government, and a system of writing

cuneiform
Sumerian writing; it was written on clay tablets

pharaoh
a ruler of ancient Egypt; pharaohs were considered gods by the Egyptians

A **civilization** is a large, complex community. It has cities, an organized government, and a system of writing. Its people make a living doing many different things. The first civilizations began about 5,000 years ago.

Mesopotamia. The first civilization began in Southwest Asia in the area between the Tigris and Euphrates Rivers. This area, called Mesopotamia, is now part of Iraq.

The early people of this area were the Sumerians. They built up the riverbanks to prevent the rivers from flooding. They built canals to bring water to faraway fields. They invented bronze by mixing copper and tin. Bronze is a very hard metal that was made into strong tools and weapons. The Sumerians had a system of writing called **cuneiform**. They also had a system of counting.

Egypt. Around the same time, the Egyptian civilization was developing in North Africa. Egypt was located in the Nile River Valley. The Nile's floods brought rich soil to the farmlands.

The Egyptians had a strong government headed by a **pharaoh**. When a pharaoh died, his or her body was preserved as a mummy. The mummy was placed in a huge tomb called a pyramid. The ruler's riches were buried, too. The Egyptians did this for religious reasons. They wanted to make sure the pharaoh would have what was needed in the afterlife.

Ancient Egyptians built many pyramids.

China. Around the same time that Sumer and Egypt began, civilization developed in China. The Chinese civilization was located along the Yellow River, where the soil was good for farming. The river provided water and transportation.

China did not have much contact with other ancient civilizations. It is surrounded by **natural barriers**. Mountains, deserts, and oceans protect it. The Chinese called their land the Middle Kingdom. They believed it was the center of the world.

The Chinese invented many things. They made fine pottery and silk. They made weapons and items out of bronze. Their writing system had about 3,000 characters. Each character stood for a word instead of a sound.

Greece. Ancient Greece was not like the river civilizations of Mesopotamia, Egypt, and China. Greece is mountainous, so much of its land is not good for farming. Greece is surrounded by the Mediterranean Sea. Thus, many Greeks fished or traded for a living. Unlike the river civilizations, the Greeks did not have a civilization ruled by one person. Instead, there were many **city-states**, each with its own ruler. Athens was one important city-state.

In Athens, a new form of government arose. Citizens voted at public meetings to make laws. This was the first democracy. However, slaves and women were not citizens. They could not vote.

Ancient Greeks built many outdoor theaters to show plays. They also loved sports. They created the Olympic Games, which first took place in ancient Greece.

natural barrier
a landform or body of water that is hard to cross; it protects an area from enemy attack

city-state
a political unit made up of a city, its people, and the surrounding countryside

The ancient Greeks loved sports. This statue is of a discus thrower.

republic
a country whose leader is chosen by the people

empire
when a central power rules many different lands and peoples

Romans built this aqueduct to bring water to Segovia, Spain. It is still in use.

convert
to adopt a different religion

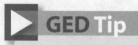

GED Tip

When you read history passages on the GED Social Studies Test, pay attention to dates. This will help you understand the order of events.

Rome. In Italy, the small city-state of Rome set itself up as a **republic** in 509 B.C. In a republic, people elect leaders. The leaders then run the government.

For the next few hundred years, Rome's armies conquered many lands. First, Rome gained control of Italy. Then they conquered all the lands around the Mediterranean Sea. This expansion weakened the republic. The army was fighting so many wars, the men didn't have time to take care of their lands. In 49 B.C., a general named Julius Caesar took control of Rome. The next ruler, Augustus, made himself emperor. The Republic was over. Rome became an **empire**. The Roman Empire lasted for several hundred years.

The Romans were great builders. They built roads, bridges, and aqueducts. Some of these are still used today. In addition, the Romans developed a system of law. They set up ways to make trials fair. Roman law became the basis for later legal systems in Europe.

West Africa. Several civilizations developed in West Africa. These civilizations were based on trade. The first of these civilizations was the kingdom of Ghana, which began around A.D. 400. Ghana took over the gold mines of West Africa. They traded gold for salt from North Africa. Starting in the 700s, traders from North Africa brought Islam to Ghana.

In the 1200s, Ghana fell into decline, or started losing power. The next civilization to take power was the empire of Mali. The rulers of Mali **converted** to Islam, the religion of the North African traders. The empire of Mali lasted until the 1400s.

The next West African civilization was Songhai. It was the largest empire of West Africa. Scholars from all over the Islamic world studied at one of its main cities, Timbuktu.

Practice

Vocabulary ■ **Write the word or words that best complete each sentence.**

1. During its early years, Rome was a _____ .

2. Mountains and deserts were _____ that protected ancient China.

3. The _____ of Egypt were buried in large tombs called pyramids.

natural barriers

pharaohs

cuneiform

republic

Understanding Time Order ■ **Circle the number of the correct answer.**

4. Which was the most recent West African civilization?

   (1) the kingdom of Ghana

   (2) the empire of Mali

   (3) the empire of Songhai

   (4) the empire of Egypt

5. Augustus ended the Roman Republic. After that, Rome was

   (1) a city-state.

   (2) an empire.

   (3) a collection of villages.

   (4) a nation.

Comparing and Contrasting ■ **Circle the number of the correct answer.**

6. How were ancient Mesopotamia, Egypt, and China alike?

   (1) They all had the same writing system.

   (2) They all were ruled by pharaohs.

   (3) They all made fine pottery and silk.

   (4) They all developed in river valleys.

Check your answers on page 166.

invade
to enter an area in order to take it over, usually by force

Middle Ages
the period between 500 and 1350 in Europe; feudalism was the political system, and the Catholic Church had much power

feudalism
a political system in which landowners let others use their land in exchange for loyalty and military service

noble
in the Middle Ages, a landowner; also called a lord

knight
in the Middle Ages, a noble who fought on horseback for his lord

The Roman Empire was able to keep order in Europe until the 300s. Then the great empire weakened, and it was **invaded**. The Franks, a Germanic tribe that became the French, attacked from the north. The Vandals, another Germanic tribe, attacked from the south. The Huns, a Mongolian tribe, attacked from the east. By A.D. 500, the Roman Empire had fallen apart. There was no strong government to keep order in Europe. People no longer felt safe.

As a result, a new political system arose during the **Middle Ages**. This system was called **feudalism**. The local **nobles**, or lords, ruled. They owned the land. The lords would give land to weaker lords, or vassals. In return, the vassals promised to fight for the lords.

A lord's gift of land included the people who farmed the land. These people were called peasants. Peasants also served in the lord's army. In addition, they grew food for everyone.

During the Middle Ages, small wars were common. Lords fought each other with small armies of **knights** and built strong stone castles for protection. When an attack was expected, everyone moved behind the castle walls. The castle was easier to defend than the farms and fields.

During the Middle Ages, nobles built castles to protect themselves and their people from attack.

Feudalism divided Europe into many small units. In contrast, the Catholic Church brought Europe together during the Middle Ages. The Church controlled much of the land. Many Catholic priests were also feudal lords. The Church had its own government, laws, courts, and taxes.

At this time, few people could read and write. But Catholic priests and monks were educated. They all spoke, read, and wrote Latin. Some of them served as advisors to lords. Others copied and studied ancient books. They kept some of the knowledge of the ancient world alive.

In 1095, the **pope** called for the first **Crusade**. Lords and knights from all over Europe went to Southwest Asia. They wanted to take control of Jerusalem. This city was considered holy. European Christians defeated the Muslims who ruled Jerusalem. Europeans ruled the city for a short time, but Muslims regained Jerusalem within 100 years. The Crusades continued, but Europeans never won back Jerusalem. Although the Crusades were a military failure, Europeans brought back new ideas and goods from Asia.

During the 1300s, the **Renaissance** began in Florence, Italy. Renaissance means "rebirth." From 1350 to 1600, Europe was "reborn." Feudalism began to disappear. Strong kings and strong nations took its place. During this time, there were many advances in the arts and sciences.

pope
the leader of the Catholic Church

Crusade
a war by the Catholic Church against Muslims for control of the city of Jerusalem

Renaissance
the period from 1350 to 1600 in Europe, when people became interested again in ancient Greece and Rome and art and science

GED Tip

Some questions on the GED Social Studies Test are based on historic maps or pieces of art. These pictures show important details about history.

This historic map of Florence, Italy, was made in 1490.

Lady Ermine *by Leonardo da Vinci shows the beauty and realism of Renaissance art.*

During the Renaissance, artists studied art from ancient Greece and Rome. They studied the human body and nature. They developed new methods for painting. Using what they learned, Renaissance artists created a beautiful new style of art.

Renaissance scholars studied the ancient world. One Renaissance scholar, Petrarch, traveled all over Europe during the 1300s. He looked for old writings. He found forgotten books by ancient Greeks, Romans, and early Christians. These old writings contained many important ideas.

Renaissance writers wrote books, too. For example, Machiavelli wrote a book for rulers. He wrote about how to gain and hold on to power. Another writer, Bruni, wrote about history. Bruni also translated many writings of the ancient Greeks.

The printing press was invented in the 1400s. Before that, books were copied by hand. This was time-consuming, so books were rare. The printing press allowed books to be printed by the hundreds. Printed books quickly spread both old and new ideas across Europe.

By the 1500s, many people were upset with the Catholic Church. They felt it was too concerned with wealth and power. In 1517, a monk named Martin Luther posted a list at a church in Germany. This list named the problems many people had with the Church. Within days, Luther's list was printed. Within weeks, it had spread across Europe. Luther's beliefs helped spark the **Protestant Reformation**. People who protested some of the actions and teachings of the Catholic Church became Protestant Christians.

Protestant Reformation
a movement within the Catholic Church that caused some people to break away from Catholicism; Protestant churches formed as a result

Martin Luther

Practice

Vocabulary ■ Write the word or words that best complete each sentence.

1. During the _____ , a lord protected his land and people in return for their service.

2. A _____ served his lord by fighting for him on horseback.

3. During the _____ , people studied the art and ideas of the ancient Greeks and Romans.

knight

pope

Renaissance

Middle Ages

Understanding Cause and Effect ■ Circle the number of the correct answer.

4. What led to the rise of feudalism in Europe?

   (1) the lack of a strong government to keep people safe
   (2) the spread of Christianity in Europe
   (3) advances in building and farming
   (4) the rise of strong kings and strong nations

5. What was a result of the invention of the printing press?

   (1) Latin became the language of the Church.
   (2) Priests and monks copied ancient books.
   (3) Renaissance art became more realistic.
   (4) Books became more common, and ideas spread rapidly.

Making Inferences ■ Circle the number of the correct answer.

6. Where were farms and fields located during the Middle Ages?

   (1) in towns
   (2) outside the castle walls
   (3) inside the castle
   (4) on land that peasants owned

Check your answers on page 167.

In Great Britain, yarn and cloth were made in homes during the 1500s and 1600s. A merchant gave a family raw wool and cotton. Members of the family usually worked together. They cleaned the fibers. They spun it into yarn by hand. They wove the yarn into cloth on hand looms. When the cloth was made, the family gave it to the merchant. He paid them by the piece or by the yard.

As Great Britain's population grew, the **demand** for cloth also grew. The system of making cloth in homes could not keep up with the demand. So **inventors** figured out ways to spin and weave faster.

The first invention was the flying shuttle. It speeded up weaving. With the flying shuttle, weavers could weave much faster than spinners could make yarn. The next invention was called the spinning jenny, which made several threads at once.

One invention led to another. Soon the machines were very big and too expensive for families to buy. In addition, the machines ran on water power. So merchants built textile mills next to rivers and streams. These mills held the large machines for spinning yarn and weaving cloth.

demand
the amount of goods or services that people want to buy

inventor
a person who creates a new machine or a new way of doing something

New machines made yarn and cloth much faster than spinners and weavers working by hand.

Families could no longer make a living by weaving cloth at home. Instead, many people started working in the mills. There they ran the machines that made yarn and cloth. In this new **factory system**, people were paid daily or weekly for their work. These payments were called wages.

This change in how cloth was made was the start of the **Industrial Revolution**. During the Industrial Revolution, machines were used to make many goods that before had been made by hand. At first, these machines were powered by running water. Later, they were powered by steam engines.

The Industrial Revolution changed the way people in Great Britain lived. Until then, most people had lived on farms or in small villages. With the Industrial Revolution, more people began moving to the towns and cities. They could get jobs in the mills there.

Cities grew very fast during the Industrial Revolution. For example, Manchester, England, had about 16,000 people in 1750. Then textile mills were built there. By 1850, the population was 455,000. Such fast growth caused problems. There was not enough housing and clean water. People threw sewage and garbage into the streets, so disease was common. Because wages were low, children often had to work to help their families.

factory system
a system in which workers and machines are brought together in one place to make goods

Industrial Revolution
the period when the economy changed so that most goods were made by machine rather than by hand

Manchester, England, was an overcrowded industrial city in the 1800s.

Despite these problems, the Industrial Revolution created riches for some. It made Great Britain the most powerful nation in the world. The Industrial Revolution spread from Great Britain to the rest of Europe and the United States. In the 1800s, Europe became the manufacturing center of the world. Soon, European nations were competing to buy raw materials to make goods. They were also competing to sell their goods overseas.

The European nations wanted to make sure they could buy and sell what they needed. So they established colonies overseas. The colonies provided raw materials such as metals and cotton. The colonies bought manufactured goods such as tools and cloth.

imperialism
the taking over of a country or region by another country

Imperialism occurs when one country takes over the government or the economy of another country or region. The years from 1870 to 1914 are called the Age of European Imperialism.

During the Age of Imperialism, Europe controlled most of Africa and Asia. Great Britain had the largest empire. Its colonies included Egypt, South Africa, and India. By the time World War I started in 1914, the European nations had many overseas colonies to protect.

GED Tip

On the GED Test, a chart may give details to support the main point of a passage. Read charts and passages together to find main ideas and supporting details.

The Number of Colonies Held by European Nations, 1900		
European Nation	**Number of Colonies in Africa**	**Number of Colonies in Asia**
Belgium	1	0
France	5	1
Germany	4	1
Great Britain	16	8
the Netherlands	0	5
Portugal	2	1

Practice

Vocabulary ■ **Write the word or words that best complete each sentence.**

1. Changes in the way cloth was manufactured set off the _____ in Great Britain.

2. During the Age of _____ , Europe controlled most of Africa and Asia.

Industrial Revolution

demand

Imperialism

Comparing and Contrasting ■ **Write your answer.**

3. How did the system of making cloth at home differ from the factory system of making cloth?

_____

_____

_____

_____

_____

Understanding Cause and Effect ■ **Circle the number of the correct answer.**

4. What caused the British demand for cloth to increase during the 1700s?

   (1) The quality of cloth was not as good.
   (2) Cloth became very expensive.
   (3) The population of Britain increased.
   (4) The amount of cotton and wool increased.

5. What was the result of European competition for raw materials in the late 1800s?

   (1) the independence of the 13 American colonies
   (2) the formation of European colonies in Africa and Asia
   (3) an increase in cooperation among nations
   (4) the start of the Cold War between the United States and the Soviet Union

Check your answers on page 167.

nationalism
strong feelings of pride and loyalty for one's country

alliance
a group of nations that agree to help one another during a war

trench
a ditch dug by soldiers for protection

There was much tension among European nations from 1900 to 1914. Feelings of **nationalism** ran high. There were conflicts over overseas colonies. Sometimes these conflicts almost led to war. For this reason, the nations of Europe built up their armies.

European nations also formed **alliances**. Members of an alliance are called allies. European allies promised to help one another if a war broke out. By 1914, there were two main alliances in Europe. The first was the Central Powers—Germany, Austria-Hungary, and the Ottoman Empire. The second was the Allied Powers—Great Britain, France, and Russia.

If two nations in different alliances declared war on each other, many other nations would be drawn into the war. And that's just what happened. In 1914, a Serbian man shot an Austro-Hungarian leader. Austria-Hungary declared war on Serbia. Serbia was allied with Russia, so Russia then declared war on Austria-Hungary. Soon, most of Europe was at war. World War I had begun.

Germany invaded Belgium and northern France. There the Germans were stopped by Allied forces. Both armies settled into long lines of trenches. For three years, they fought from the **trenches**. Millions of soldiers died.

During World War I, soldiers dug trenches. They ate, slept, and fought in the trenches.

During the war, twenty more nations joined the Allies. These nations included the United States and Japan. By 1918, the Allies defeated Germany and the Central Powers.

During the next 20 years, **dictators** took over governments in many parts of the world. In Italy, Benito Mussolini rose to power. Germany was taken over by Adolf Hitler, who began the Nazi party. After the end of World War I, Germany, Italy, and Japan became allies.

dictator
a person who has complete control over a nation

In the late 1930s, Italy and Germany took over some nearby regions. Japan invaded China. The democracies of Europe did not stop them. However, in 1939, Germany invaded Poland. As a result, Great Britain and France declared war on Germany and its allies. World War II began.

The Axis powers fought the Allies in this war. Germany, Italy, and Japan were the Axis powers. The Allies included Great Britain, the Soviet Union, and the United States.

World War II in Europe

By 1942, Germany and Italy had taken over most of Europe and North Africa. Only Great Britain and the Soviet Union had not fallen. Japan had taken over most of East Asia and many islands in the Pacific Ocean.

After 1942, the Allies began to advance on the Axis powers. They took back North Africa. They took back the Pacific, island by island. In June 1944, the Allies invaded Europe. They defeated Germany in May 1945. Three months later, the United States dropped two atomic bombs on Japan. As a result, Japan **surrendered** on August 14, 1945.

World War II had reached around the world. Most countries were affected by the war. More than 50 million people died worldwide. Many of them were not soldiers. They were **civilians**, or people who are not in the military.

After the war, European nations lost their empires. Most of their colonies became independent nations. In contrast, the United States and the Soviet Union came out of the war as superpowers. For almost 50 years, they competed with one another in the Cold War. When the Soviet Union collapsed in 1991, the Cold War ended.

After World War II, a new kind of warfare, called **terrorism**, spread. In terrorism, small political groups perform violent acts. They try to get what they want by attacking civilians. They want to show that the nations under attack cannot protect their own citizens. They get **publicity** for their causes.

Many nations have been the victims of terrorist attacks. Northern Ireland, Israel, Germany, Spain, India, Pakistan, Indonesia, Russia, and the Philippines have all been attacked by various groups. On September 11, 2001, the United States was also attacked by terrorists. More than 3,000 people died. That terrorist attack was a turning point. The United States and its allies began a war on terrorism.

surrender
to give up to an enemy

civilian
someone living in a country who is not in its military

terrorism
a violent act against civilians intended to weaken the power of a government

publicity
getting public attention through the news media

GED Tip

History passages may describe causes and effects. Paying attention to causes and their effects can help you answer questions on the GED Test. Look for clue words that signal cause and effect as you read.

Practice

Vocabulary ▪ Write the word that best completes each sentence.

1. An _____ is a group of nations that help one another during a war.

2. A strong feeling of pride in one's country is called _____.

3. Many people killed during World War II were _____.

4. Since 2001, the United States has fought a war on _____.

civilians
dictators
terrorism
nationalism
alliance

Reading a Map ▪ Look at the map on page 115. Circle the number of the correct answer.

5. Which of these nations had come under Axis control by 1941?

   (1) Estonia
   (2) France
   (3) Great Britain
   (4) Spain

Understanding Cause and Effect ▪ Circle the number of the correct answer.

6. In 1939, Germany invaded Poland. This resulted in

   (1) an alliance with Great Britain.
   (2) a dictator taking over the government of Germany.
   (3) an agreement that Germany could rule Poland.
   (4) Great Britain and France declaring war on Germany.

7. Japan surrendered in August 1945 because

   (1) it controlled many Pacific Islands.
   (2) it needed to stop fighting the Allies and aid Germany.
   (3) two atomic bombs were dropped on the country.
   (4) the Soviet Union invaded Japan.

Check your answers on page 167.

Reading Bar Graphs

A bar graph compares numerical information. You need to be able to understand what a bar graph shows. You also need to be able to find specific information, or data, in a bar graph.

The title tells you what the graph shows. The labels list the data being compared. You use the labels to find data.

 Strategy Look at the graph. Ask yourself: What is the title? What do the labels say?

1. Look for the title. This is in large letters above the graph.

2. Read the labels. There are labels on the vertical axis, or the line going up and down. There are labels on the horizontal axis, or the line going across.

Minority Soldiers Who Were Drafted During World War II

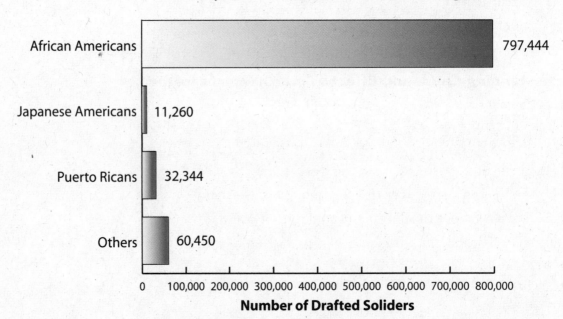

Exercise 1: **Look at the graph above. Complete the sentences.**

1. This graph shows _____ during World War II.

2. The horizontal axis shows _____ .

Strategy Look at the bars. Ask yourself:
How do the bars compare? Which bar is the longest?
Which is the shortest?

1. The length of a bar shows an amount. A long
   bar shows a greater amount than a short bar.

2. Figure out what amount a bar represents. Read the
   bar's label on the horizontal axis. Then read the label
   on the vertical axis to see the amount.

Exercise 2: Look at the bar graph below. Write *T* for true or *F* for false next to each statement.

_____ **1.** The United States made about 60,000 army tanks
during World War II.

_____ **2.** Great Britain made more army tanks during World
War II than the Soviet Union did.

_____ **3.** Of the four nations shown, Germany made the
fewest army tanks.

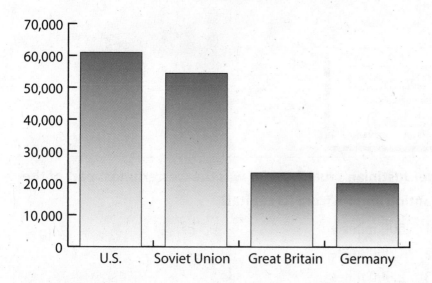

Army Tank Production During World War II

Check your answers on page 168.

Understanding Passages and Graphics Together

The GED Social Studies Test often has questions based on both passages and graphics. To answer the questions, you must combine information from the passage and the graphic.

 Strategy Try the strategy on the example below. Use these steps.

Step 1 Read the title. What is the topic?

Step 2 Read the paragraph. What is the main idea?

Step 3 Read the question. Look again at both the graphic and paragraph to find the information you need.

When the western Roman Empire collapsed in the 400s, the eastern Empire continued. It was called the Byzantine Empire. Its capital was Constantinople. Justinian ruled as emperor there from 527 to 565. Under his rule, the Byzantine Empire reached its largest size.

Byzantine Empire, A.D. 565

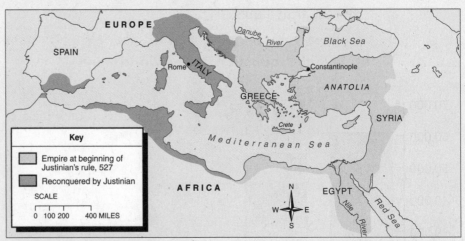

Under Justinian's rule, how far was the westernmost part of the Byzantine Empire from its capital?

(1) 500 miles

(2) 1,000 miles

(3) 2,000 miles

(4) 3,000 miles

Practice

In Step 1 you read the map title. The map shows the Byzantine Empire in the year 565. In Step 2 you read the paragraph. It describes the Byzantine Empire under the Emperor Justinian. In Step 3 you answered the question. In the paragraph, you found that Constantinople was the capital. Using the map scale, you found the distance. The correct answer is Choice (3). The western border of the empire is about 2,000 miles from Constantinople.

Practice the strategy. Use the steps you learned. Circle the number of the correct answer.

As nations build more factories, more jobs can be found in industrialized areas. After World War II, African nations started building more factories. African cities grew much faster than the farming areas. For example, the city of Lagos grew quickly after the war.

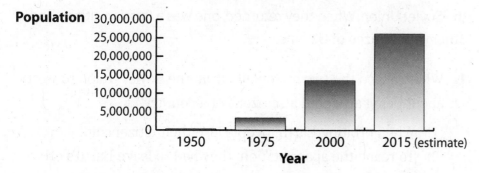

Population of Lagos, Nigeria

1. What does the information in the paragraph and bar graph tell you about Nigeria?

   (1) Overall, the population of Nigeria has decreased since 1950.
   (2) After 1950, many Nigerians moved to Lagos to find work.
   (3) Nigeria is the most industrialized nation in Africa.
   (4) Lagos is the largest city in Nigeria.

Check your answers on page 168.

Read each passage and question carefully. Circle the number of the correct answer.

Questions 1–2 are based on the following passage.

In 1991, the Soviet Union sent two astronauts to its space station. The space station, named *Mir*, orbited Earth. The first astronaut was in space for ten months. The second astronaut joined him after five months. During their stay on *Mir*, the Soviet Union collapsed. Russia and a number of other nations were formed from it.

On *Mir*, the astronauts realized that their nation no longer existed. There were strikes at the space center base on Earth that guides space missions. The astronauts worried that they might not be able to get back to Earth. They were afraid that when they got there, they would not be accepted as citizens of any country.

Workers at the space center brought the astronauts safely back to Earth. When they left on their mission, both had been citizens of the Soviet Union. When they returned, one was a Russian citizen. The other was a citizen of Ukraine.

1. What caused the two astronauts from the Soviet Union to worry about being accepted as citizens of a country?

   (1) When orbiting Earth, people lose their citizenship.
   (2) To reach the space station, they had to leave Earth's orbit.
   (3) The Soviet Union collapsed while they were on *Mir*.
   (4) Workers at their space center went on strike.

2. What can you infer about these astronauts?

   (1) They opposed the changes that took place in the Soviet Union in 1991.
   (2) They wanted to spend more time on *Mir*.
   (3) They were poorly trained for their space mission.
   (4) They came from different parts of the Soviet Union.

Questions 3–5 are based on the following bar graph.

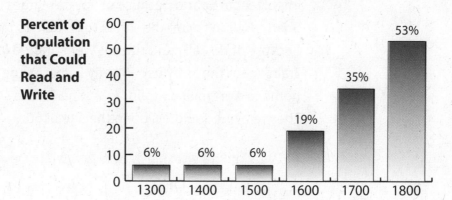

Literacy in England, 1300–1800

3. What percent of the English population could read and write in 1600?

   (1) 6%
   (2) 19%
   (3) 35%
   (4) 53%

4. What is the main idea shown by this bar graph?

   (1) The literacy of the English population increased from 1300 to 1800.
   (2) In 1300, less than 10 percent of the English population could read and write.
   (3) A population that can read and write is a national resource.
   (4) In 1800, more than half the English population could read and write.

5. From the data in the bar graph, what can you tell about life in England from 1300 to 1500?

   (1) Reading and writing were important skills.
   (2) All children were taught to read.
   (3) All children had to go to school until age 16.
   (4) Few people needed to read and write for their work.

Questions 6–7 are based on the following paragraph.

Sparta was a city-state in ancient Greece. The military was very important in Sparta because of Sparta's large slave population. Spartans didn't want the slaves to be able to take over the city-state. Because of this, all male citizens were drafted into the Spartan army. Training for the army began early in life. At age 7, Spartan boys left home to start military training. At age 20, they entered the army. They remained soldiers up to the age of 60.

6. Why did all citizens of Sparta have to become soldiers?

    (1) Sparta needed to prevent its slaves from taking over.

    (2) Boys and men had to be physically fit and strong.

    (3) Only citizens could vote for Spartan leaders.

    (4) Spartan homes were too small for male children.

7. What can you infer about the Spartan army?

    (1) Volunteer soldiers became army leaders.

    (2) Most residents of Sparta belonged to the army.

    (3) Women and men fought side by side in the army.

    (4) The army was well-trained and effective.

Check your answers on page 168.

Unit 4 Skill Check-Up Chart

Check your answers. In the first column, circle the numbers of any questions that you missed. Then look across the rows to see the skills you need to review and the pages where you can find each skill.

Question	Skill	Pages
1, 6	Understanding Cause and Effect	Unit 2, 56–57
2, 5, 7	Making Inferences	Unit 3, 90–91
3, 4	Reading Bar Graphs	118–119

Unit 5   Economics

In this unit you will learn about

- trading goods and services
- budgeting, debt, and the U.S. economy

barter

mortgage

deflation

income

Economics is the study of resources, or things that are used to make goods and to provide services for people. Economics is also the study of how people pay for goods and services.

List a job you have had.

_____

_____

Resources are limited, so people have to decide how best to use them. We can't have everything, so we have to make economic choices. We have to choose what to buy and what not to buy.

What is something you bought recently? Why did you buy it?

_____

_____

Lesson 19   Trading Goods and Services

Trade began before history was recorded. People traded things that they made or grew for things that they needed. For example, people might have traded food and clay pots for wool cloth.

Things you trade are called goods. Services, such as washing clothes or cutting someone's hair, can be traded, too. Exchanging goods or services for other goods or services is called **bartering**.

bartering
trading without using money

Trade became easier when money was invented. The first money used was probably shells, stones, or beads. Later people began to use metal bars and coins. Then paper money was invented. It made trading even easier. Paper bills are easier to carry than large amounts of metal or coins. Look at the timeline below.

1200 B.C.	1000 B.C.	500 B.C.	A.D. 800	Today
Cowrie shells	Iron and lead coins	Silver and gold coins	Paper money	Credit cards Debit cards

Everything we produce and trade has a money value. The money value is the price. Price depends on both the supply of goods or services and how much people are willing to pay for them.

law of supply and demand
the relationship between the supply of goods and the consumer's demand for them

The rise and fall of prices is known as the **law of supply and demand**. For example, fruits and vegetables cost more in the winter. That's because they're in shorter supply in the winter than in the summer. When there are **shortages** of goods, prices go up. Then businesses try to make more goods. As a result, the supply of goods increases. Then the prices start to come down.

shortage
not enough of something to meet demand

Sometimes, prices for everything rise over a period of years. This is called **inflation**. Inflation affects your buying power, or how much your money will buy. When prices go up, items cost more. You must spend more to buy the same things. For example, in 1960 people could buy a large bag of potato chips for 49 cents. Today, that same bag of chips costs $2.99.

inflation
when prices of goods and services keep increasing, and the value of money keeps decreasing

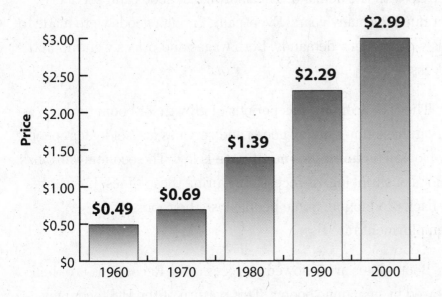

Price of Large Bag of Potato Chips, 1960–2000

GED Tip

When you see a bar graph on the GED Social Studies Test, pay attention to the title. The title tells you the main idea of the graph and what the graph shows.

As inflation continues, money buys less and less. People need to earn more money. If wages don't keep up with the rate of inflation, people can't buy as much. Business slows down. Companies cut back and people lose their jobs. This is called a **recession**.

recession
a decline in economic activity

If a recession goes on long enough, it turns into a **depression**. Banks and businesses close. Millions of people lose their jobs. Many people can't pay their rent or mortgage, and they lose their homes.

depression
a long period of economic decline

The last depression in the United States took place in the 1930s. It was called the Great Depression. From 1929 to 1933, prices actually fell by 50 percent. This was the only period of **deflation** we have had in the last hundred years. World War II helped bring the country out of the Great Depression.

deflation
when prices of goods and services keep falling, and the value of money keeps rising

Wars cause great changes in supply and demand. Wars may create jobs. Wars may also cause shortages, which lead to higher prices. People have money to spend, but there are fewer things to buy. That is because the factories make mostly war supplies.

After World War II, there was a shortage of cars, houses, and other goods. As a result, more workers were hired. More people worked overtime to make enough goods. As people earned more money, they bought more things. The production of goods couldn't keep up with the demand. The shortage of goods and services continued for many years. Eventually, enough goods were made to satisfy consumers' demands. Both wages and prices went up in the process.

The U.S. economy has periods of growth, or boom times. During these times, many goods and services are sold. Most people have jobs. The **unemployment rate** is low. The economy also has periods of shrinking, or recession. During these times, businesses cut back production. Some people lose their jobs. The unemployment rate rises.

Boom times are followed by recessions. Recessions are then followed by economic booms. This pattern of the U.S. economy is called the **business cycle.**

unemployment rate
the percentage of workers who are looking for jobs but cannot find them

business cycle
the pattern of the U.S. economy where periods of economic growth are followed by periods of economic slowdown

The Business Cycle

Practice

Vocabulary ■ Write the word that best completes each sentence.

1. If a recession lasts a long time and gets worse, it can become
   a _____ .

2. During a period of _____ , prices and
   wages rise.

3. When there is a _____ of a product,
   the price of that product will probably go up.

shortage

depression

bartering

inflation

**Understanding Time Order ■ Circle the number of the
correct answer.**

4. What was the earliest form of money?

   (1) paper money
   (2) coins made of lead and iron
   (3) coins made of silver and gold
   (4) shells

5. According to the business cycle diagram on page 128, what usually
   follows the end of a recession?

   (1) a depression
   (2) a period of growth
   (3) a period of deflation
   (4) a period of decreasing economic activity

Comparing and Contrasting ■ Write your answer.

6. Compare the unemployment rate during a boom time and during
   a recession.

   _____

   _____

   _____

Check your answers on page 169.

Drawing Conclusions

When you read about economics, you need to draw conclusions. A conclusion is a judgment. You make this judgment after studying all the facts you have. Often conclusions are not stated in a paragraph. Instead, you have to draw your own conclusions.

Suppose you read this in the newspaper: *The number of jobs for healthcare workers will double in the next 20 years.* You might conclude that a career in healthcare would be a good idea.

 Strategy Study the facts. Think about what they might mean. Ask yourself: What conclusion can I draw from these facts?

1. Read the paragraph. Note the facts.
2. Think about what the facts might mean.
3. Draw a conclusion based on the facts.

Exercise 1: Read the paragraph. Think about the facts.

During the 1920s, stock prices rose. People who owned stocks got rich. Then in October 1929, stock prices dropped sharply. They continued to fall for more than a year. Many people had put all of their savings into stocks. The value of their stocks was almost worthless. They were left with little or no savings.

Read the paragraph above again. Then choose the best conclusion. Circle the number of the correct answer.

What can you conclude about owning stocks?

(1) Owning stock is a sure way to get rich.
(2) Owning stock can be risky.
(3) People who own stocks will lose all of their money.

Many stocks are bought and sold in markets called exchanges. This is the New York Stock Exchange.

Strategy A good conclusion is backed up by facts. To check your conclusion, ask yourself: What facts support this conclusion?

1. Go over the facts in the passage.
2. Check to make sure that the facts support the conclusion.

Exercise 2: Read the paragraph. Underline the facts. Then answer the questions below.

One cause of changes in demand for goods is changes in technology. For example, DVD players came on the market in the 1990s. They were a good substitute for VCRs. The demand for DVD players increased. As a result, the demand for VCRs dropped.

1. What conclusion can you draw about the role of technology in changing demand for products?

   _____

   _____

   _____

   _____

2. What facts did you base this conclusion on?

   _____

   _____

   _____

   _____

Check your answers on page 169.

Lesson 20   Budgets, Debt, and the U.S. Economy

budget
a plan for how to save and spend money

income
money coming into a household, a business, or a government

expense
a cost involved in running a household, a business, or a government

Office of Management and Budget
a government agency that manages the money the government collects

People often set up **budgets** to plan how to use their money. A budget is a monthly plan of **income** and **expenses**. For a family, most income usually comes from wages. Some income may also come from social security payments. A family's expenses may include rent, food, clothing, utilities, entertainment, and other costs. When income is greater than expenses, the family can save the extra money. These savings may later pay for college, a car, a trip, a house, retirement, or other future needs.

Businesses must budget, too. Businesses want to make a profit, so they try to keep their expenses lower than their income. Businesses try to save part of their profit for the future. They may want to use some of their profit to build new facilities, hire new people, or buy new equipment.

Governments also have budgets. The U.S. government has an **Office of Management and Budget** (OMB). The president asks the OMB to help prepare a budget for the coming year. This budget goes to Congress for approval. Congress votes on how to spend the money. It chooses which federal programs will receive money and decides how much money each program will get.

How a Typical 2003 Federal Dollar Was Spent

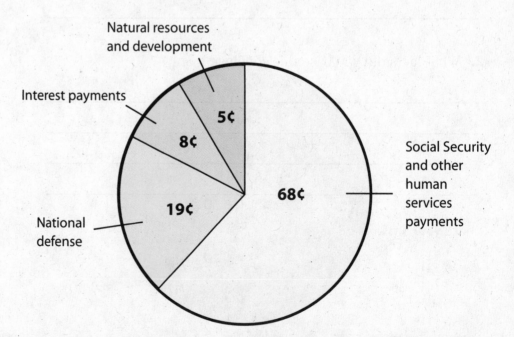

Natural resources and development

Interest payments

5¢

8¢

68¢

19¢

National defense

Social Security and other human services payments

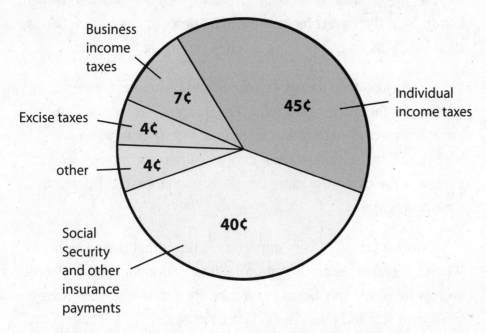

Where a Typical 2003 Federal Dollar Came From

Business income taxes — 7¢

Excise taxes — 4¢

other — 4¢

Individual income taxes — 45¢

Social Security and other insurance payments — 40¢

The government's income comes from taxes. Congress votes on the next year's spending program before the tax money actually comes in. Sometimes the tax money turns out to be more than the amount of money Congress voted to spend. Then there is a budget **surplus**. There was a budget surplus from 1997 to 2001.

Sometimes the tax money turns out to be less than the amount Congress voted to spend. Then there is a budget **deficit**. The federal government usually has a budget deficit.

To get the money to pay its expenses, the government borrows money. It does this by issuing **bonds**. Buyers of the bonds lend the government money. In return, the government pays them **interest**.

The interest rate that the government pays affects interest rates throughout the economy. The government interest rate is controlled by the **Federal Reserve System**. The Federal Reserve is like a national bank. It can raise the interest rate it charges other banks to borrow money. When this happens, all interest rates tend to rise. The Federal Reserve can also lower the interest it charges. When this happens, all interest rates tend to fall.

surplus
when the government gets more money in taxes than it spends

deficit
when the government spends more than it gets in taxes

bond
a certificate of debt that says the loan plus interest will be repaid within a certain period of time

interest
the amount of money paid on a loan or earned on money in a bank

Federal Reserve System
the U.S. national banking system that sets government interest rates

Banks compete with the government for people's money. If banks pay less interest than the government, people will not put their money in savings accounts. Instead, they will buy government bonds. So if the government is paying 4 percent interest on bonds, then banks also pay 4 percent interest on savings accounts.

Banks also lend money to people and businesses. They charge interest on the money they lend. The interest rate banks charge on loans is always greater than the interest rate they pay on savings accounts. For example, a bank may pay 4 percent interest on a savings account. At the same time, it may charge 6 or 7 percent for a **mortgage**.

mortgage
a loan used to buy a house or other building

Interest rates are very important. They affect the economy. When interest rates are low, it costs little to borrow money. People borrow money to buy houses and cars. Businesses borrow money to expand and add jobs. The economy grows.

When interest rates are high, the economy slows down. People borrow less and buy less. Businesses also borrow less. The rate of inflation might drop. If the economy slows down too much, however, a recession can occur. Then many people lose their jobs.

GED Tip

Examples can help you understand main ideas on the GED Social Studies Test. Look for words like *for example* or *for instance* to signal an example.

The Federal Reserve uses its power to set interest rates to influence the economy. For example, when it wants the economy to grow, it lowers its interest rate. When it wants the economy to slow down, it raises its interest rate.

Consumer Debt

People borrow money for large purchases such as a house or a car. They also borrow money when they use a credit card. People sometimes owe more money than they can repay. Then they may declare bankruptcy. In bankruptcy, people pay some debts. Other debts are "forgiven," and people don't have to pay them. After a few years, debtors can start over.

Practice

Vocabulary in Context ■ Write the word that best completes each sentence.

1. Before opening a savings account, people check to see which banks pay the most _____ .

2. A _____ helps people manage their money.

3. Most people get their _____ from wages or social security payments.

> bond
>
> budget
>
> income
>
> interest

Drawing Conclusions ■ Circle the number of the correct answer.

4. What can you conclude about the federal budget process?

  (1) The budget process is very precise and accurate.

  (2) The budget process is based on estimates.

  (3) Politics play no part in the budget process.

  (4) The budget process is controlled by the president.

Understanding Time Order ■ Circle the number of the correct answer.

5. The Office of Management and Budget (OMB) prepares a budget for the coming year

  (1) after the president has asked for a new budget.

  (2) after Congress votes on how to spend money.

  (3) after all the taxes have been collected.

  (4) after taxes have been collected, but before Congress votes.

6. Bank interest rates usually go up

  (1) before the Federal Reserve interest rate goes up.

  (2) after the Federal Reserve interest rate goes up.

  (3) when banks have a lot of customers.

  (4) before banks issue mortgages.

Check your answers on page 169.

Reading Circle Graphs

A circle graph shows the parts of a whole. The circle represents the whole of something. Each wedge is a part. You need to be able to understand what a circle graph shows. You also need to be able to find specific data in a circle graph.

The title tells you what the graph shows. The labels tell you the data being compared. You use the labels to find data.

> **Strategy** Look at the circle graph. Ask yourself: What is the title? What do the labels say?
>
> 1. Read the title. The title tells what the graph shows.
>
> 2. Read the labels. There are labels for each part of the circle. They tell you what each part of the graph stands for.

Jay and Dina's Monthly Income

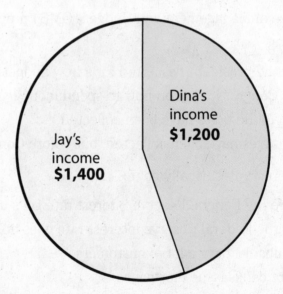

Exercise 1: Look at the circle graph above. Complete the sentences.

1. This graph shows _____ .

2. Dina makes _____ each month.

Strategy Look at the parts of the circle graph. Ask yourself: What does the size of each part mean?

1. A part represents an amount that is a piece of a whole. Read the labels to figure out how much a part represents.

2. Compare the size of a part to the size of the whole circle and to the other parts. A large part shows a greater amount than a small part does.

Exercise 2: Look at the circle graph below. Write _T_ for true or _F_ for false next to each statement.

_____ **1.** Jay and Dina's largest monthly expense relates to their car.

_____ **2.** Jay and Dina budget about $215 a month for health insurance.

_____ **3.** Jay and Dina budget about $825 a month for rent and savings.

_____ **4.** Jay and Dina budget more for utilities and phone than for groceries.

Jay and Dina's Monthly Budget

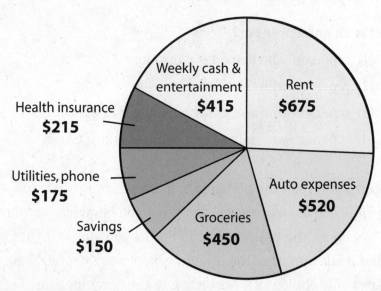

Weekly cash & entertainment **$415**

Rent **$675**

Health insurance **$215**

Utilities, phone **$175**

Savings **$150**

Groceries **$450**

Auto expenses **$520**

Check your answers on page 170.

Choosing the Right Answer

All the questions on the GED Social Studies Test are multiple-choice questions. You need to recognize the correct answer.

To answer a GED question, read the passage or graphic. Then read the question. Read each answer choice, choosing the best answer.

 Strategy Try the strategy on the example below. Use these steps.

Step 1 Read the passage or graphic.

Step 2 Read the question. Read each answer choice.

Step 3 Eliminate any wrong choices. Then choose the best answer.

Step 4 Check the passage or graphic again. Make sure the answer you chose is correct and the other answers are wrong.

Example

An entrepreneur has the ability to combine resources in a way that will make money. Entrepreneurs recognize a new business opportunity. They raise money to open a new business. They hire managers and workers to help them run the business.

What is an entrepreneur?

(1) a person who manages a business

(2) a person who starts a new business

(3) a person who works for a manager in a business

(4) a person who buys new products and services

In Step 1 you read the paragraph. In Step 2 you read the question and each answer choice. In Step 3 you eliminated wrong choices. You chose the best answer. In Step 4 you checked your answer and made sure that the other answers were wrong. The correct answer is choice (2). According to the paragraph, an entrepreneur is someone who starts a new business.

Practice

Practice the strategy. Use the steps you learned. Circle the number of the correct answer.

In the early 1900s, Henry Ford set up an assembly line to make cars in his factory. On an assembly line, a product moves from one worker to the next. Each worker has a special job to do on the product. Before Ford's assembly line, one worker would build a car. It would take more than twelve hours. The assembly line cut the time to make a car to only an hour and a half.

1. What effect did the assembly line have on manufacturing a car?

   (1) The time needed to make a car decreased sharply.

   (2) The time needed to make a car increased sharply.

   (3) The time stayed the same, but the number of workers increased.

   (4) The time stayed the same, but the number of workers decreased.

Practice the strategy with a graphic. Use the steps you learned. Circle the number of the correct answer.

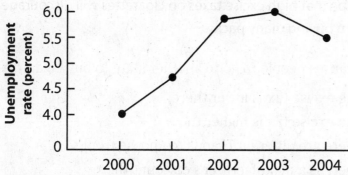

U.S. Unemployment Rate, 2000–2004

2. In which year was the unemployment rate the highest?

   (1) 2001

   (2) 2002

   (3) 2003

   (4) 2004

Check your answers on page 170.

Read each passage and question carefully. Circle the number of the correct answer.

Questions 1–2 are based on the following passage.

Excise taxes are sales taxes on specific products and services. For example, there are excise taxes on gasoline and tires. There are also excise taxes on cigarettes, wine, beer, liquor, and phone calls.

Both the federal government and state governments collect excise taxes. States often tax items at different rates. For example, New Jersey may charge a $2.40 excise tax per pack of cigarettes. Neighboring Pennsylvania may charge only a $1.35 excise tax. As a result, many New Jersey residents will drive to Pennsylvania to buy cigarettes.

The main purpose of excise taxes is to raise money for government use. But some excise taxes have another purpose. That purpose is to reduce sales of the item. For example, cigarette excise taxes are very high. The government set these high taxes to help pay for costly health problems caused by cigarette smoking. Government officials hope that high excise taxes on cigarettes will discourage people from buying many packs.

1. What causes people to go to another state to buy cigarettes?

   (1) The excise tax is lower there.
   (2) The excise tax is higher there.
   (3) There are different brands to choose from.
   (4) There is a manufacturer's discount there.

2. Based on the passage, what can you conclude would be a way for the government to cut fuel consumption?

   (1) Charge a federal sales tax on all products.
   (2) Lower the excise tax on automobiles.
   (3) Lower the excise tax on gasoline and other fuels.
   (4) Raise the excise tax on gasoline and other fuels.

Questions 3–5 are based on the following circle graph.

Budget of the U.S. Department of Homeland Security, 2004

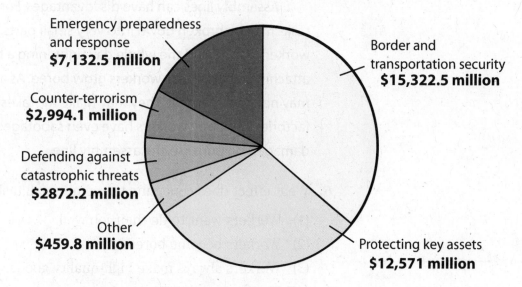

Emergency preparedness and response
$7,132.5 million

Border and transportation security
$15,322.5 million

Counter-terrorism
$2,994.1 million

Defending against catastrophic threats
$2872.2 million

Other
$459.8 million

Protecting key assets
$12,571 million

3. What is the topic of this circle graph?

   (1) the amount by which the Department of Homeland Security went over budget in 2004
   (2) the 2004 budget of the Department of Homeland Security
   (3) the 2004 budget of the U.S. government
   (4) the amount budgeted for border and transportation security in 2004

4. Which part of homeland security has the greatest amount budgeted for it?

   (1) defending against catastrophic threats
   (2) counter-terrorism
   (3) protecting key assets
   (4) border and transportation security

5. From the data on the circle graph, what can you conclude is the purpose of the Department of Homeland Security?

   (1) spending tax dollars as shown in its 2004 budget
   (2) training the armed services to respond to terrorist threats
   (3) preventing and responding to terrorism in the United States
   (4) preventing and responding to terrorism overseas

Questions 6–7 are based on the following paragraph.

Assembly lines can have disadvantages. For example, the tasks may be broken down into very small parts. Some workers may spend the whole day tightening a bolt or attaching a part. These workers grow bored. As a result, they may not pay attention. They may make mistakes. In some factories, unhappy workers have even sabotaged, or damaged on purpose, the assembly line.

6. What effect does repeating the same small task have?

(1) Workers want to do their job well.

(2) Workers become bored.

(3) Workers always make high-quality goods.

(4) Workers earn more money.

7. Based on the passage, what can you conclude about how a good assembly line should be set up?

(1) The tasks should be broken down into the smallest parts.

(2) The line should be slow to give workers extra time.

(3) Workers should work on larger segments of the product.

(4) The line should be speeded up to prevent boredom.

Check your answers on page 170.

Unit 5 Skill Check-Up Chart

Check your answers. In the first column, circle the numbers of any questions you missed. Then look across the rows to see the skills you need to review and the pages where you can find each skill.

Question	Skill	Page
1, 6	Understanding Cause and Effect	Unit 2, 56–57
2, 5, 7	Drawing Conclusions	130–131
3, 4	Reading Circle Graphs	136–137

Social Studies Posttest

This posttest will give you an idea of how well you have learned social studies using the skills in this book.

You will read short passages, graphs, maps, and political cartoons. You will answer multiple-choice questions based on what you have read. There is no time limit.

Read each passage and question carefully. Circle the number of the correct answer.

Question 1 is based on the following map.

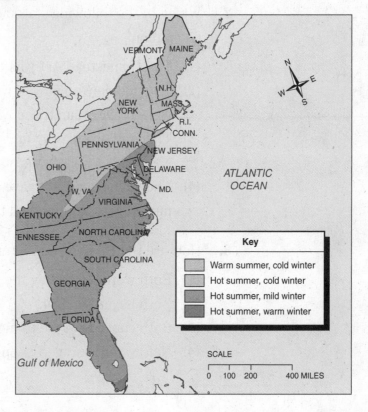

1. Which state or states has a climate with hot summers and warm winters?

    (1) South Carolina

    (2) Florida

    (3) Georgia

    (4) all states south of West Virginia

Questions 2–3 are based on the following paragraph.

In the 1800s, the U.S. government wanted people to settle in the West. The Homestead Act was passed in 1862. The Act gave 160 acres of land to anyone who moved west and worked the land for five years. People began settling Nebraska, the Dakotas, and the Kansas plains. More people went west during the Gold Rush. In 1874, 15,000 people went to the Dakotas to look for gold.

2. Which of the following statements about the Homestead Act is an opinion?

   (1) The Homestead Act was passed in 1862.
   (2) The people who moved west under the Homestead Act were braver than those who stayed in the East.
   (3) The land given away under the Homestead Act was in Nebraska, the Dakotas, and the Kansas plains.
   (4) The Homestead Act gave 160 acres of land to anyone who moved west and worked the land for five years.

3. How are the Homestead Act and the Gold Rush similar?

   (1) Both were started by the government.
   (2) Both began in 1874.
   (3) Both caused people to move west.
   (4) Neither encouraged people to settle in the West.

Questions 4–6 are based on the following bar graph.

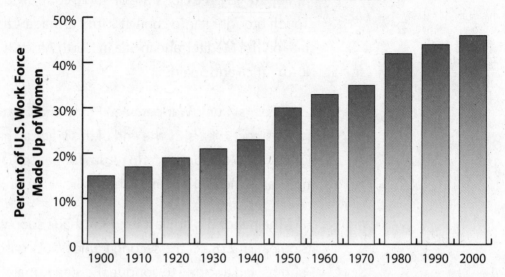

Woman Workers 1900–2000

4. During which year did women first make up more than 40 percent of the work force?

   (1) 1960
   (2) 1970
   (3) 1980
   (4) 1990

5. What can you conclude from this graph?

   (1) Occasional increases in the number of women in the work force were followed by declines.
   (2) There has been a general decrease in the number of women in the work force.
   (3) There have been a fairly steady number of women in the work force.
   (4) There has been a steady increase in the number of women in the work force.

6. What can you infer from this graph?

   (1) Women workers are paid more than men.
   (2) Most women who work finished high school.
   (3) A higher percentage of children born in 2000 have mothers who work than did children born in 1920.
   (4) Most women work part-time in low-wage jobs.

Questions 7–8 are based on the following passage.

By 264 B.C., the city-state of Rome controlled all of Italy. Rome's growth brought it into conflict with Carthage. Carthage was a city-state on the Mediterranean Sea in North Africa. It controlled trade in North Africa and Spain.

The first Punic War between Rome and Carthage began in 264 B.C. It lasted 23 years. By the end of this war, Carthage was tired of fighting. It asked for peace. In return for peace, Carthage gave Rome three large Mediterranean islands—Sicily, Sardinia, and Corsica.

The peace did not last long. Carthage soon wanted revenge for its defeat. In 218 B.C., the second Punic War began. A general named Hannibal led an army to conquer Rome. He marched through Spain and Gaul, which is known as France today. He crossed the Alps into northern Italy. Elephants carried the army's gear. In the cold mountains, all but one elephant died.

For 17 years, Hannibal's army roamed Italy. Hannibal tried to win the support of the Romans. However, most stayed loyal to Rome. Finally, Rome invaded Carthage. Hannibal had to leave Italy to defend Carthage. He was defeated in North Africa, and Carthage had to give Spain to Rome.

7. What did Rome gain after the first Punic War?

   (1) control over Italy
   (2) the islands of Sicily, Sardinia, and Corsica
   (3) Spain
   (4) the city-state of Carthage

8. What caused the second Punic War?

   (1) Hannibal marched his army across the Alps.
   (2) Rome invaded North Africa.
   (3) Carthage wanted to win back Spain.
   (4) Carthage wanted revenge for its loss in the first war.

Questions 9–11 are based on the following circle graph.

Federal Aid to State and Local Governments for U.S. Department of Agriculture Programs, 2002

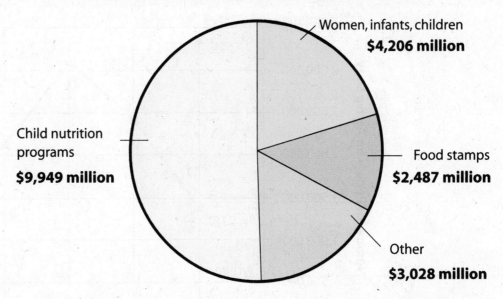

9. How much aid did state and local governments get for food stamps in 2002?
   (1) $9,949 million
   (2) $4,206 million
   (3) $3,028 million
   (4) $2,487 million

10. How did the amount for child nutrition programs compare to the amount for programs for women, infants, and children?
   (1) More than three times as much was paid for child nutrition programs.
   (2) More than twice as much was paid for child nutrition programs.
   (3) About the same amount was paid for both.
   (4) About half as much was paid for child nutrition programs.

11. From the graph, what can you conclude about federal aid for U.S. Department of Agriculture programs?
   (1) Most aid goes to California, Texas, and New York.
   (2) Most aid helps pay for food and nutrition programs.
   (3) Most aid helps farmers pay their work-related expenses.
   (4) States pay the majority of expenses for all the programs.

Questions 12–13 are based on the following line graph.

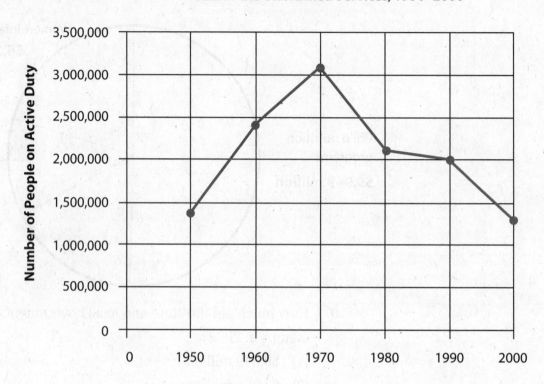

Size of the U.S. Armed Services, 1950–2000

12. What was the size of the U.S. armed services in 1980?

    (1) about 1,500,000 people
    (2) about 2,000,000 people
    (3) about 2,500,000 people
    (4) about 3,000,000 people

13. Which of the following is a correct statement about the data on the graph?

    (1) The size of the armed services has been increasing steadily since 1950.
    (2) The size of the armed services decreased steadily after 1950.
    (3) More Americans served in 1970 than in 1950 or 1990.
    (4) More Americans were killed in 1950 than in 1970 or 1990.

Questions 14–16 are based on the following cartoon.

'That was a good answer. Too bad he wasn't asked that question.'

14. Who do the man and woman represent?

    (1) American retirees
    (2) American voters
    (3) candidates for political office
    (4) the audience for TV advertising

15. When can you infer the conversation in the cartoon took place?

    (1) during the president's inaugural speech
    (2) during the president's state-of-the-union speech
    (3) during a debate between presidential candidates
    (4) on election day after the polls closed

16. Which statement represents the opinion of the cartoonist?

    (1) During presidential election campaigns, the candidates debate one another.
    (2) Debates have limited value because candidates can avoid answering questions.
    (3) Americans discuss their political opinions while watching television.
    (4) Many Americans watch political news on TV.

When you have finished the *Social Studies Posttest*, check your answers on page 171. Then look at the chart on page 150.

Skills Review Chart

This chart shows you which skills you should review. Check your answers. In the first column, circle the number of any question you missed. Then look across the row to find out which skills you should review as well as the page numbers on which you find instruction on those skills. Compare the items you circled in the *Skills Review Chart* to those you circled in the *Skills Preview Chart* to see the progress you've made.

Questions	Skill	Pages
7	Understanding Time Order	20–21
3, 10	Comparing and Contrasting	30–31
12, 13	Reading Line Graphs	36–37
8	Understanding Cause and Effect	56–57
14	Understanding Political Cartoons	62–63
2, 16	Recognizing Facts and Opinions	68–69
1	Reading Maps	80–81
6, 15	Making Inferences	90–91
4	Reading Bar Graphs	118–119
5, 11	Drawing Conclusions	130–131
9	Reading Circle Graphs	136–137

Glossary

alliance a group of nations that agree to help one another during a war. *page 114*

amendment a change or addition. *page 49*

American Revolution the war between the colonists and the English government (1775–1783). *page 18*

Arctic area surrounding the North Pole and including some of northern Europe, North America, and Asia. *page 86*

article a section of the Constitution. *page 49*

baby boom a period of increased American births (1946–1965). *page 34*

bartering trading without using money. *page 126*

bill an idea for a law that is presented to Congress. *page 54*

Bill of Rights the part of the Constitution that lists people's rights. *page 50*

blockade cutting off an area so that normal travel and trade cannot take place. *page 39*

bond a certificate of debt that says the loan plus interest will be repaid within a certain period of time. *page 133*

boom a time of rapid economic growth. *page 26*

boundary a dividing line, or border, between areas. *page 78*

boycott to protest a government or any other group by refusing to use or buy its goods. *pages 18 and 66*

branch a part or section. *page 49*

budget a plan for how to save and spend money. *page 132*

business cycle the pattern of the U.S. economy where periods of economic growth are followed by periods of economic slowdown. *page 128*

cabinet the group of people who advise the president. *page 53*

candidate a person who wants to be elected. *page 58*

capital a city where the government of a country or state is located. *page 78*

censorship the act of preventing people from expressing their views. *page 50*

census an official count of all the people in the country. *page 53*

Central America the countries between Mexico and South America. *page 82*

city-state a political unit made up of a city, its people, and the surrounding countryside. *page 103*

civilian someone living in a country who is not in its military. *page 116*

civilization a large, complex society with cities, government, and a system of writing. *page 102*

civil rights the basic rights that every citizen is entitled to. *page 64*

civil war a war between two groups of people in the same country. *page 23*

claim to take ownership. *page 14*

climate the average weather conditions in a particular place. *page 82*

Cold War the struggle between the United States and the Soviet Union (end of World War II–1989). *page 33*

colony a group of people who settle in one country but are governed by the parent country. *page 14*

communicate to talk with or share information with other people. *page 26*

communism a system of government where the state controls industry and business, and all goods are shared equally by the people. *page 33*

compass rose the symbol on a map that shows the four directions: north, east, south, and west. *page 76*

compromise an agreement in which each side gives up something. *page 49*

Confederacy the South during the Civil War. *page 23*

conquistador Spanish word for *conqueror*, or someone who defeats someone else. *page 13*

Constitution the document that sets forth the laws of the United States. *page 48*

consumer goods goods that are made for people's needs and wants. *page 32*

continent one of the seven large areas of land on the earth. *page 76*

convention a meeting at which members of a political party choose their candidates. *page 58*

convert to adopt a different religion. *page 104*

Crusade a war by the Catholic Church against Muslims for control of the city of Jerusalem. *page 107*

cuneiform Sumerian writing; it was written on clay tablets. *page 102*

debtor a person who owes money and can't pay it back. *page 16*

Declaration of Independence the colonies' formal announcement of freedom from the English government. *page 18*

declare to say publicly. *page 23*

deficit when the government spends more than it gets in taxes. *page 133*

deflation when prices of goods and services keep falling, and the value of money keeps rising. *page 127*

demand the amount of goods or services that people want to buy. *page 110*

democracy a form of government in which power is held by the people. *page 33*

demonstration a public showing of a group's feelings about an issue; for example, a march. *page 65*

depression a long period of economic decline. *pages 26 and 127*

dictator a person who has complete control over a nation. *page 115*

disabled having physical or mental difficulties. *page 66*

discriminating treating groups of people in unequal and unfair ways. *page 64*

electoral college a special group of representatives from each state who elect the president and vice-president. *page 58*

electors members of the electoral college. *page 58*

Emancipation Proclamation the document that stated all slaves would be free. *page 24*

empire when a central power rules many different lands and peoples. *page 104*

equator an imaginary line around the middle of the earth. *page 76*

executive branch the president and his or her cabinet; this branch makes sure that laws are carried out. *page 53*

expense a cost involved in running a household, a business, or a government. *page 132*

export to sell and send goods to other countries. *page 82*

factory system a system in which workers and machines are brought together in one place to make goods. *page 111*

federal government a central, national government. *page 48*

Federal Reserve System the U.S. national banking system that sets government interest rates. *page 133*

feudalism a political system in which landowners let others use their land in exchange for loyalty and military service. *page 106*

fifteenth century the years from 1401 to 1500. *page 12*

First Continental Congress the first formal meeting to discuss problems the colonists had with England. *page 18*

found to start or establish. *page 16*

free state any state where slavery wasn't allowed. *page 23*

government the method of running a country, state, or city. *page 48*

governor a person who rules an area such as a colony or a state. *page 17*

grassland a large area of grass such as a plain. *page 88*

hemisphere half of the world; *hemi-* means "half"; a sphere is a ball or a globe. *page 76*

highlands land that is higher than land near the ocean. *page 94*

House of Representatives one of the two houses of Congress. *page 52*

ice cap a permanent cover of thick ice. *page 94*

imperialism the taking over of a country or region by another country. *page 112*

import to buy and bring foreign goods into a country. *page 84*

income money coming into a household, a business, or a government. *page 132*

industrialized an area with many factories. *page 86*

Industrial Revolution the period when the economy changed so that most goods were made by machine rather than by hand. *page 111*

inflation when prices of goods and services keep increasing and the value of money keeps decreasing. *page 127*

interest the amount of money paid on a loan or earned on money in a bank. *page 133*

invade to enter an area in order to take it over, usually by force. *page 106*

inventor a person who creates a new machine or a new way of doing something. *page 110*

judicial branch the courts; the branch of government that makes sure laws are constitutional. *page 54*

key the part of a map that shows what the different lines and symbols mean. *page 76*

knight in the Middle Ages, a noble who fought on horseback for his lord. *page 106*

law of supply and demand the relationship between the supply of goods and the consumer's demand for them. *page 126*

legislative branch Congress; it has the power to make laws. *page 52*

majority rule when more than half the people agree on the laws of government. *page 50*

manufacturing making products, usually in factories. *page 22*

merchant person who buys and sells things. *page 12*

Middle Ages the period between 500 and 1350 in Europe; feudalism was the political system, and the Catholic Church had much power. *page 106*

mineral a solid substance, like iron or salt, found in the earth. *page 82*

Minutemen civilians who were ready to fight at any time. *page 18*

monsoon a wind in southern Asia; it brings heavy rains to this area each year. *page 92*

mortgage a loan used to buy a house or other building. *page 134*

nationalism strong feelings of pride and loyalty for one's country. *page 114*

natural barrier a landform or body of water that is hard to cross; it protects an area from enemy attack. *page 103*

natural resources things found in nature, such as land, water, forests, and minerals. *page 86*

New Deal the programs and laws created by Roosevelt to get the U.S. economy out of the depression. *page 27*

noble in the Middle Ages, a landowner; also called a lord. *page 106*

Northwest Passage a sea route through North America to Asia. *page 14*

Office of Management and Budget a government agency that manages the money the government collects. *page 132*

petition a formal request, usually written. *page 65*

pharaoh a ruler of ancient Egypt; pharaohs were considered gods by the Egyptians. *page 102*

Pilgrims a religious group that settled the Plymouth Colony. *page 16*

plain a large area of flat land. *page 82*

plantation a large farm on which crops are raised. *page 22*

policy the way an organization is managed; the rules of an organization. *page 66*

political party a group of people who share basic positions on political issues. *page 58*

poll a place where people vote. *page 58*

pope the leader of the Catholic Church. *page 107*

press news that is published in newspapers, magazines, radio, television or on the Internet. *page 50*

primary an election where voters choose a candidate. *page 58*

profit the amount of money a company has left after subtracting the cost of doing business. *page 26*

propose suggest. *page 27*

protest to speak out against something. *page 38*

Protestant Reformation a movement within the Catholic Church that caused some people to break away from Catholicism; Protestant churches formed as a result. *page 108*

public works projects such as roads, bridges, and dams paid for by the government for the people's use. *page 32*

publicity getting public attention through the news media. *page 116*

rain forest a wet tropical forest with tall trees that grow very close together. *page 84*

ratify to formally approve. *page 66*

raw material a natural substance, like cotton or wood, from which goods are made. *page 84*

rebel a person who fights against an established government or authority. *page 38*

recession a decline in economic activity. *page 127*

reform an effort to improve. *page 40*

refugees people who flee a place because of disaster or war. *page 38*

Renaissance the period from 1350 to 1600 in Europe, when people became interested again in ancient Greece and Rome and art and science. *page 107*

representative a person who voices the needs, wants, and opinions of a group of people. *page 48*

republic a country whose leader is chosen by the people. *pages 40 and 104*

revolt to fight against authority. *page 40*

route way. *page 12*

satellite an object sent into space to circle Earth. *page 33*

scale a line that helps the reader measure distances on the map. *page 78*

secede to leave a group or organization officially. *page 23*

Second World War World War II, fought between England, the United States, and their allies on one side and Germany, Italy, Japan, and their allies on the other (1939–1945). *page 32*

segregation social separation of different groups of people. *pages 24 and 64*

Senate one of the two houses of Congress. *page 52*

settle to make home. *page 12*

shortage not enough of something to meet demand. *page 126*

Social Security a government insurance program that pays retired and disabled workers and their families. *page 28*

stock a share that a person owns in a company. *page 26*

stock market the place where stocks are bought and sold. *page 26*

surplus when the government gets more money in taxes than it spends. *page 133*

surrender to give up to an enemy. *pages 18 and 116*

symbol a picture that stands for something else. *page 60*

system of checks and balances the system that keeps the different branches of government from becoming too powerful. *page 54*

term the period of time for which a person holds office. *page 59*

terrorism a violent act against civilians intended to weaken the power of a government. *page 116*

tourism the business of providing services for people who are traveling for pleasure. *page 82*

trade to exchange goods for other goods. *page 12*

trading post a store set up by merchants or traders. *page 16*

trench a ditch dug by soldiers for protection. *page 114*

unconstitutional not following the Constitution. *page 54*

unemployment rate the percentage of workers who are looking for jobs but cannot find them. *page 128*

Union the North during the Civil War. *page 23*

veto the power of a president to reject a bill. *page 54*

welfare money given by the government to people who need help. *page 32*

Answers and Explanations

Social Studies Pretest, *pages 3–9*

Page 3

1. **(2) 58,209** According to the bar graph, choice (1) is the number of casualties in the Korean War. Choice (3) is the number of casualties in World War I. Choice (4) is the number of casualties in World War II.

2. **(1) There were over triple the deaths in World War II.** Choice (2) is incorrect because there were many more than twice the number of deaths in World War II as in World War I—405,399 compared to 116,516. Choice (3) is incorrect because there were more deaths in World War II than in World War I, not fewer. Choice (4) is incorrect because the number of deaths in the two wars was very different.

Page 4

3. **(3) The executive branch carries out the law, and the judicial branch decides matters of law.** Choice (1) is incorrect because the Supreme Court makes decisions on laws, and the president is head of the branch that carries out the laws. Choices (2) and (4) are incorrect because the executive branch carries out the law, and the judicial branch decides matters of law.

4. **(3) The president should talk to leaders of Congress before choosing a Supreme Court justice.** Congress must approve the president's choices for justices. For this reason, it might be wise for the president to discuss possible choices for Supreme Court justices with leaders of Congress. Then, a huge conflict over choices might be avoided. Choices (1), (2), and (4) incorrect because they are facts stated in the passage.

Page 5

5. **(4) The president, Congress, and the Supreme Court may not always agree.** You can conclude that the three branches may not always agree because their purposes are different. In addition, each may check the other, which leads to disagreements. Choice (1) is incorrect because the system of checks and balances keeps any one branch from becoming more powerful than the others. Choice (2) is incorrect because Congress may sometimes vote against a president's choice for a Supreme Court justice. Choice (3) is incorrect because the legislative and judicial branches have powers the president does not have, so the president cannot control them.

6. **(1) Republicans** With 232 representatives, the Republicans held more than half the seats in the House of Representatives. Therefore, they had the majority. Choices (2) and (3) are incorrect because the Democrats and the Independent held less than half of the seats in Congress. Choice (4) is incorrect because the Republican party had a majority.

Page 6

7. **(3) Metals come from the middle and western parts of Montana.** The symbol for metals appears on the middle and western parts of the map. Choice (1) is

incorrect because lettuce and strawberries are not shown on the map. Choice (2) is incorrect because poultry and wheat come from different areas. Choice (4) is not true because cattle are shown in many parts of the state and hogs in just one area.

8. **(4) It has many farms and ranches.** Since Montana's products include wheat, corn, cattle, sheep, and hogs, you can conclude there must be many farms and ranches in the state. Choices (1), (2), and (3) are incorrect because the map does not show factories, tourist attractions, or cities.

9. **(2) Montana is rich in resources.** The many product symbols scattered throughout the Montana map show that the state has many resources. Choice (1) is incorrect because the map does not give information about how much money is made in lumber and ranching. Choice (3) is incorrect because the map does not tell about working conditions for miners. Choice (4) is incorrect because the map does not give any information about the cities of Montana.

Page 7

10. **(1) Hitler wanted to expand German territory.** Since the passage explains that Hitler wanted to expand German territory, it is logical that invading Poland was an effort to do this. Choice (2) is incorrect because nothing in the passage indicates that Poland had a dictator. Choices (3) and (4) are incorrect because invading Poland didn't help Japan or Italy.

11. **(4) Japan attacked Pearl Harbor.** The third paragraph explains that the United States stayed out of the war until 1941, when Pearl Harbor was attacked. Choices (1) and (3) are incorrect because these events happened after the United States entered the war. Choice (2) took place two years before the United States entered the war.

12. **(2) when Japan surrendered.** The fourth paragraph explains that Japan's surrender ended the war. The other choices took place before the end of the war.

Page 8

13. **(1) 4,000,000** Find 1790 on the horizontal axis. The point on the line above it represents the population that year. Read across to the vertical axis to see how many people there were. Choices (2), (3), and (4) are incorrect because the population was less than 10,000,000 in 1790.

14. **(3) The U.S. population grew slowly at first and then very rapidly.** As the slope of the line shows, between 1790 and 1830 the population went from 4,000,000 to about 13,000,000. That was a slow increase. From 1830 to 1890, the population went from about 13,000,000 to more than 60,000,000. That was a rapid increase, as the slope of the line shows. Choice (1) gives the opposite rate of growth shown. Choice (2) is incorrect because the population increased. Choice (4) is incorrect because the graph gives no information about immigration.

Page 9

15. **(2) the nation being buried by the money it owes** The man in the cartoon represents the United States, as you can see from the label on the man's hat. The

leaves represent the huge national debt, as you can see from the label on the leaves. The debt has grown so high that the man can't rake his way out debt. The other choices are not represented by the labels in the cartoon.

16. **(4) A large national debt is difficult to keep up with.** The cartoonist shows this by burying the United States up to the neck in debt. Choice (1) is a fact unrelated to the topic of the cartoon. Choice (2) is a fact about the national debt. Choice (3) is an opinion unrelated to the topic of the cartoon.

Unit 1 Lesson 1

Page 15

1. merchant
3. conquistador
2. claim
4. Northwest Passage

5. **(3) a trip by ship would be easier and faster.** Choice (1) is incorrect because the main goal was to buy and trade goods faster. Choice (2) is incorrect because they could already get there by land. Choice (4) is incorrect because they did not know the Americas existed.

6. the Incas
7. the Indies

Lesson 2

Page 19

1. Debtors
3. American Revolution
2. Minutemen
4. surrendered

5. **(2) wanted to be free to practice their religion.** Choice (1) is incorrect because governors and merchants got rich in the colonies. Choice (3) is incorrect because debtors were sent to the colonies as a

punishment. Choice (4) is incorrect because merchants owned trading posts in the colonies.

6. **(1) raised taxes on some products.** Choice (2) is incorrect because the colonists welcomed trade with England. Choice (3) is incorrect because the colonists boycotted England's goods, not the other way around. Choice (4) is incorrect because some debtors already lived in the colonies.

7. the Declaration of Independence
8. George Washington

GED Skill Strategy, *pages 20–21*

Page 20

Exercise 1: <u>In 1492</u>, <u>first</u>, <u>After</u>, <u>in 1505</u>, <u>later</u>

Page 21

Exercise 2: (2) Choice (2) is correct because these events happened over seven years in a specific order. Choice (1) does not involve time order.

Exercise 3: There are many ways to answer the question. Here is an example.

For seven years, Columbus tried to find someone to pay for his trips. First, he asked John II of Portugal for money. After that, he wrote to Henry VI of England. Finally, he met with Spain's Queen Isabella.

Lesson 3

Page 25

1. free states
2. civil war

3. **(1) after seven Southern states seceded from the Union.** Choice (2) is incorrect because the Emancipation

Proclamation was issued after the Confederacy was set up. Choice (3) is incorrect because the Confederacy ended when the Civil War ended. Choice (4) is incorrect because the Confederacy was set up in 1860 and the slaves were freed in 1863.

4. **(2) during the Civil War.** Choice (1) is incorrect because the Emancipation Proclamation was issued in 1863 and the war began in 1861. Choice (3) is incorrect because the Confederacy did not surrender until 1865. Choice (4) is incorrect because Lincoln was not President during the 1850s.

5. **(3) for almost another hundred years after the Civil War.** Choices (1) and (2) are incorrect because these dates mark the beginning and end of the Civil War. Choice (4) is incorrect because this event did not end segregation.

6. **(1) slave states.** Choices (2), (3), and (4) are incorrect because none of the free states joined the Confederacy. These free states were the Northern, or the Union states.

Lesson 4

Page 29

1. stock   2. boom   3. depression

4. **(1) after the stock market crash of 1929.** Choices (2) and (4) are incorrect because both were responses to the Great Depression. Choice (3) is incorrect because the Great Depression began in 1929.

5. **(3) during the Great Depression.** Choices (1) and (4) are incorrect because Roosevelt told voters he had a plan to help end the Great Depression. Choice (2) is incorrect because Black Tuesday was the day of the stock market crash that began the depression in the United States.

6. **(3) hired people to work on government projects.** Choices (1), (2), and (4) are incorrect because jobs programs did not watch over stock trading, set minimum wages, or provide unemployment insurance.

GED Skill Strategy, *pages 30–31*

Page 30

Exercise 1: 1. same, as   **2.** unlike

Page 31

Exercise 2: Roosevelt's New Deal was (like) a rope thrown to drowning people. Government began to play a role in people's lives (more) than ever before. The government created a safety net to help protect Americans against hard times. Some Americans think Roosevelt was one of the (best) presidents the United States has ever had.

Exercise 3: There are many possible ways to answer the question. Here are two examples.

- During the Great Depression, many people went without food and had no place to live. Though Americans experience homelessness and hunger today, it is not as bad as it was then.

- More people are employed today than during the Great Depression. Back then, about 13 million Americans were without jobs.

Lesson 5

Page 35

1. Welfare   2. communism

3. **(1) the United States felt threatened by the Soviets.** Choice (2) is incorrect because the United States and the Soviet

Union did not work together after the war. Choices (3) and (4) are incorrect because the Soviet Union was not the most powerful nation in the world.

4. **(3) their cities, factories, and farms had been destroyed.** Choice (1) is incorrect because the Americans did not force them to rebuild. Choice (2) is incorrect because Europe and Japan were weak because of the war's destruction. Choice (4) is incorrect because selling goods was not the main reason for rebuilding.

5. **(2) after the war, many Americans started families.** Choices (1) and (3) are incorrect because neither would cause a population increase. Choice (4) is incorrect because the government did not encourage people to have children.

GED Skill Strategy, *pages 36–37*

Page 36
Exercise 1:
1. the number of TV sets   2. 1970, 2000

Page 37
Exercise 2:
1. T   2. F   3. T

Lesson 6

Page 41
1. protested   2. blockade   3. revolted
4. **(2) when Gorbachev resigned from office.** Choices (1), (3), and (4) all happened before the end of the Soviet Union.

5. **(2) communism fell in East Germany.** Choices (1), (3), and (4) took place before the Berlin Wall was torn down.

6. **(3) sending war supplies.** According to the passage, choices (1), (2), and (4) did not take place.

GED Test-Taking Strategy

Page 43
1. **(3) The French had few colonists and towns.** Choices (1) and (2) describe ways the French colonies were similar to the English and Spanish colonies. Choice (4) does not describe French colonies.

Unit 1 GED Test Practice, *pages 44–46*

Page 44
1. **(3) Washington was elected president.** Choices (1), (2), and (4) all took place after Washington became president.

2. **(2) Congress discussed how to address Washington.** Choices (1) and (4) took place before Washington's speech. Choice (3) did not take place right after the speech.

3. **(1) They are more formal than "Mr. President".** Choices (2), (3), and (4) are not true since "Mr. President" is simpler, shorter, and more democratic than the more formal titles.

Page 45
4. **(3) 4 million** Choice (1) is the approximate population in 1830. Choice (2) is the approximate population in 1850. Choice (4) is incorrect because the graph does not show a time when the slave population was over 4 million.

5. **(2) in 1810** Choice (1) is incorrect because the graph does not give information about the slave population before 1800. Choices (3) and (4) are incorrect because the slave population was much higher than 1 million in these years.

6. **(1) It increased.** Choices (2) through (4) are incorrect because the line slopes upward.

Page 46

7. **(4) The Montgomery bus boycott began.** Choices (1), (2), and (3) took place before Rosa Parks was arrested.

8. **(4) wanted to be treated as equals.** Choice (1) is incorrect because Brown was the only one of the three to address segregation in public schools. Choice (2) is incorrect because Parks was the only one of the three to cause a boycott. Choice (3) is incorrect because Robinson was the only one of the three to be the first African American to hold a particular job.

Unit 2 Lesson 7

Page 51

1. censorship
2. Constitution
3. amendments
4. third
5. first
6. second

7. **(1) People of a country should have the power to make their own laws.** Choice (2) is incorrect because the authors of the Constitution believed that the government's powers needed to be limited. Choice (3) is incorrect because federal laws need to be stronger than state laws to hold the country together. Choice (4) is not mentioned in the text as a basis for the Constitution.

8. **(3) Each branch could keep the other two from becoming too powerful.** Choice (1) is incorrect because the amount of work to do was not an issue. Choice (2) is incorrect because the issue of who would govern was not a factor in this decision. Choice (4) is incorrect because the branches do not represent regions of the country.

Lesson 8

Page 55

1. Senate   2. veto   3. judicial

4. **(2) after the census is taken.** Choice (1) is incorrect because the census must be taken first to determine the number of people to be represented. Choice (3) is incorrect because the census must be completed. Choice (4) is incorrect because the census is taken once every ten years.

5. **(2) after the President appoints them.** Choice (1) is incorrect because they must be appointed first. Choices (3) and (4) are incorrect because they must be approved before they can serve.

6. Your answer should include two of the following: The Senate has 100 members. In contrast, the House has 435 members. There are two senators from each state. However, the number of representatives in the House depends on each state's population. Senators are elected for six-year terms. Representatives are elected for two-year terms.

GED Skill Strategy, *pages 56–57*

Page 56

Exercise 1: The key word *so* should be underlined.

Exercise 2:

cause: the Constitution was carefully written

effect: it is still a useful plan of government today.

Page 57

Exercise 3:

1. yes   **2.** yes

Exercise 4: There are several ways to rewrite these sentences. Here is an example. The underlined words show cause and effect.

The president chose a new judge for a federal court. Since the Senate agreed with the president's choice, it voted in favor of the judge. As a result, the judge was appointed to the federal court for life.

Lesson 9

Page 61

1. candidate, primary   **3.** symbols

2. terms

4. (2) People vote in a primary election. Choices (1), (3), and (4) are incorrect because they take place after the primary elections are completed.

5. (4) young adults aged 18 to 20 Choices (1), (2), and (3) are incorrect because these groups all got the right to vote before young adults.

6. (4) a change in the state's population Choice (1) is incorrect because primaries are used to choose candidates to run for election. Choices (2) and (3) are incorrect because the number of Democrats and Republicans does not affect the number of

electors in the electoral college.

GED Skill Strategy, *pages 62–63*

Page 62

Exercise 1:

1. The people are a married couple. They represent regular American citizens.

2. They are talking about the negative things candidates do to get elected. They are also talking about what a "nice" election would be like.

Page 63

Exercise 2:

1. Your answer will be either yes or no depending on what you've seen.

2. Answers will vary. Here is an example.

People complain about negative ads because they do not tell about problems and issues. They just tell bad things about the other candidate.

3. Answers will vary. Here is an example.

Candidates use negative ads to get the attention of voters. According to the man in the cartoon, "nice" ads and campaigns are boring.

Lesson 10

Page 67

1. petition **2.** segregation   **3.** policy

4. (2) The Fourteenth Amendment to the Constitution. Choice (1) is incorrect because the 1875 decision restored legal segregation. Choice (3) is incorrect because this amendment gave African American men the right to vote. Choice (4) is incorrect because the bus boycott occurred in the 1950s, long after African Americans had won citizenship.

5. **(1)** Petitions and demonstrations are both ways to get the attention of the government in order to bring about changes. Both methods are nonviolent.

   (2) A petition is a document requesting something. Many people sign it. In contrast, a demonstration is a public gathering of many people who are concerned about an issue.

GED Skill Strategy, *pages 68–69*

Page 68

Exercise 1: The words *felt*, *believed*, and *believe* should be underlined.

Page 69

Exercise 2:
 1. F   2. O   3. F   4. O   5. O   6. F

Exercise 3: There are many possible ways to complete the exercise. Here is an example.

Fact 1: The First Amendment gives all people the right to speak freely.

Fact 2: The First Amendment gives people the right to print their views.

Opinion: The First Amendment should not allow newspapers to print news that might harm the nation's defense.

GED Test-Taking Strategy

Page 71

1. **(4) People accused of crimes have Sixth Amendment rights.** Choices (1), (2), and (3) are details, not the main idea.

2. **(3) Overview of State Legislatures** Choices (1) and (2) are incorrect because they focus on details from the paragraphs. Choice (4) is incorrect because the passage describes only one branch of state government—the legislative branch.

3. **(2) They serve only part-time in the legislature.** Choices (1) and (3) are incorrect because wanting a higher office has nothing to do with working at a regular job. Choice (4) is incorrect because their legislative jobs are just part-time.

Unit 2 GED Test Practice, *pages 72–74*

Page 72

1. **(3) Congress would vote for president and vice president.** Choices (1), (2), and (4) are incorrect because a tie in the electoral college sends the election decision to Congress.

2. **(2) Both candidates got the same number of votes.** Choice (1) is not a reason for the legislature to get involved in an election. Choices (3) and (4) are incorrect because they are not true.

3. **(4) Pulling a name from a hat is a poor way to break a tie vote.** Choices (1), (2), and (3) are incorrect since they are facts, not opinions.

Page 73

4. **(1) one man trying to get another man to vote** Choice (2) is incorrect because the short man is certainly not an election worker; he is not interested in voting. Choice (3) is incorrect because there are no instructions on voting in the cartoon. Choice (4) is incorrect because the two

men are talking about voting, not about a particular political candidate.

5. **(3) a voter** Choices (1) and (2) are incorrect because nothing indicates the short man is a politician from either party. Choice (4) is incorrect because poll workers would already be at the polls.

6. **(3) Voters don't care enough to vote.** Choices (1), (2), and (4) are incorrect because they are facts, not the opinion of the cartoonist.

Page 74

7. **(2) Washington's limiting himself to two terms as president** Choice (1) is incorrect because the Constitution originally set no limits on the number of terms a president could serve. Choice (3) is incorrect because Roosevelt's presidency broke the two-term tradition. Choice (4) is incorrect because the amendment made the two-term limit into a law, not a tradition.

8. **(4) Four terms is too many for a president to serve.** Choices (1), (2), and (3) are incorrect because they are all facts, not beliefs. You can check that each of these facts is true.

Unit 3 Lesson 11

Page 79

1. key   2. continents   3. boundary

4. **(1) the oceans.** Choices (2),(3), and (4) are incorrect because they cover less area.

5. **(2) The earth's land is divided into continents.** Choice (1) is incorrect because water covers three fourths of the earth's surface. Choice (3) is incorrect because a globe shows the whole earth.

Choice (4) is incorrect because there are seven continents.

6. **(3) The best type of map is a road map.** Choices (1), (2), and (4) are incorrect because they are facts. You can check them.

GED Skill Strategy, *pages 80–81*

Page 80

Exercise 1:

1. 4,500   **2.** 2,000

Page 81

Exercise 2:

1. hot and wet; desert; warm summers and cool or cold winters

2. desert

3. **(2) along the northern coast.** Choice (1) is incorrect because central Australia has a desert climate. Choices (3) and (4) are incorrect because the southern coast is not considered a wet climate.

Lesson 12

Page 85

1. export   **2.** plains   **3.** climate

4. Chile and Argentina

5. the Mississippi River

6. Guatemala, Belize, El Salvador, Honduras, Nicaragua, Costa Rica, Panama

7. the Pacific Ocean

These are many possible ways to answer the question. Here is an example.

8. Both Canada and the United States have good farmland. Both have enough rain for farming. Both manufacture many goods.

Lesson 13

Page 89

1. grassland   2. industrialized   3. Arctic
4. Uganda, Tanzania, Kenya   5. Tanzania

These are many possible ways to answer the question. Here is an example.

6. Many places in Africa do not have good soil. Many places do not get enough rain. Farming is difficult in Africa. In contrast, Europe has rich soil and good rainfall. Europe grows a lot of food, and farming is not difficult there.

GED Skill Strategy, *pages 90–91*

Page 90

Exercise 1: Europe and the United States are about the same size. Europe's population is double that of the United States.

Exercise 2: (1) There are more people per square mile in Europe than in the United States. Choices (2) and (3) are incorrect because if Europe and the United States are about the same size and more people live in Europe, then Europe must be more crowded.

Page 91

Exercise 3: There are many possible ways to answer the question. Here is an example.

Deserts do not get much rain. Deserts are hot during the day. Without water in the desert, people get thirsty and plants die.

Farmers need a dependable amount of rain to grow food.

Exercise 4: (3) Large parts of Africa cannot be farmed. Choice (1) is incorrect because deserts, which do not get much rain and are therefore not suited for farming, cover a large portion of Africa. Choice (2) is incorrect because deserts would not have a problem with floods. Choice (4) is incorrect because the passage does not support the choice. There are many possible ways to answer the question. Here is an example.

Exercise 5: More than two fifths of Africa is desert.

Lesson 14

Page 95

1. monsoon   2. ice cap
3. the Atlantic Ocean, the Pacific Ocean, the Indian Ocean
4. the South Pole
5. **(4) dress in different types of clothing.** Choices (1), (2), and (3) are incorrect because the large size and varying climates of Asia mean that the people who live in different areas differ in the foods they eat, the crops they raise, and the types of homes they have.
6. **(1) not very populated.** Choices (2), (3), and (4) are incorrect since the central and western parts of the country are unlikely to be either crowded or noisy if most of the people live along the east coast. Therefore, it is also unlikely that these areas will be filled with shopping malls or be important business centers.

GED Test-Taking Strategy

Page 97

1. **(3) Elevation can be shown in different ways on maps.** Choices (1) and (4) are incorrect because they are details and do not describe the general topic of

the diagram. Choice (2) is incorrect because it is an opinion, not the main idea of the diagrams.

2. **(4) facts about the people of the Dominican Republic and Haiti** Choices (1), (2), and (3) are incorrect because the table does not show natural resources, political systems, or physical features.

Unit 3 GED Test Practice, *pages 98–100*

Page 98

1. **(4) The land is high and flat and less likely to flood.** Choices (1) and (2) describe the Amazon lowlands. Choice (3) is incorrect because deep valleys are not good for farming.

2. **(3) by boat** Choices (1) and (2) are incorrect because these types of vehicles would have difficulty passing through a region covered by a rain forest. Choice (4) is incorrect because it would be too difficult to transport a lot of goods by foot.

Page 99

3. **(2) the climate in Europe and Asia** Choice (1) is incorrect because the map shows the Eastern Hemisphere. Choices (3) and (4) are incorrect because the map shows climate areas, not political boundaries or landforms.

4. **(3) southwest Asia** Choice (1) is incorrect because the map indicates that Europe has medium rainfall. Choice (2) is incorrect because the map indicates that the climate varies in the mountains of South Asia. Choice (4) is incorrect because the map indicates that the climate of southeast Asia is hot and wet.

5. **(1) clothing that keeps you warm** Choice (2) is incorrect because there is little rain in northern Asia. Choice (3) is incorrect because northern Asia is cold, and you need warm clothing there. Choice (4) is incorrect because dust storms are more likely in the desert rather than the cold climate of northern Asia.

Page 100

6. **(4) The river provides water for drinking and farming.** Choices (1), (2), and (3) are incorrect because people tend to live in places because they can meet their basic needs there. These include having fresh water and being able to grow food to eat or to sell.

7. **(3) Very few people live there.** Choices (1) and (4) are incorrect because a desert is not the best place for farming. Choice (2) is incorrect because a desert has less water than a river valley.

Unit 4 Lesson 15

Page 105

1. republic   2. natural barriers   3. pharaohs

4. **(3) the empire of Songhai** Choices (1) and (2) are incorrect because the empires of Ghana and Mali came before the empire of Songhai. Choice (4) is incorrect because Egypt is in northeast Africa.

5. **(2) an empire.** Choices (1) and (3) are incorrect because Rome was far larger than a city-state or group of villages after Augustus. Choice (4) is incorrect because Rome was made up of many lands and peoples.

6. (4) They all developed in river valleys. Choice (1) is incorrect because the three civilizations had different writing systems. Choice (2) is incorrect because only Egypt was ruled by pharaohs. Choice (3) is incorrect because only China was known for its fine pottery and silk.

Lesson 16

Page 109

1. Middle Ages 2. knight 3. Renaissance

4. **(1) the lack of a strong government to keep people safe** Choices (2) through (4) are incorrect because feudalism evolved when people needed law and order after the collapse of the Roman Empire.

5. **(4) Books became more common, and ideas spread rapidly.** Choice (1) is incorrect because Latin was already the language of the Catholic Church. Choice (2) is incorrect because the printing press replaced the priests and monks copying ancient books. Choice (3) is incorrect because the printing press did not affect art.

6. **(2) outside the castle walls** Choice (1) is incorrect because there was no space for farms and fields inside the towns. Choice (3) is incorrect because there was no space for farms and fields inside the castle walls. Choice (4) is incorrect because the land was owned by the lord, not the peasants.

Lesson 17

Page 113

1. Industrial Revolution 2. Imperialism

3. There are many ways to answer this question. Here is an example:
When cloth was made at home, family members worked together. They spun yarn and wove cloth by hand. They were paid by the piece or by the yard. In a factory, large machines were gathered in one place. Workers came to the factory to operate the machines, which produced yarn and cloth very quickly. Workers were paid daily or weekly wages.

4. **(3) The population of Britain increased.** Choice (1) is incorrect because decreased quality would not lead to increased demand. Choice (2) is incorrect because higher prices would decrease demand. Choice (4) is incorrect because the amount of cotton and wool would not increase demand for cloth.

5. **(2) the formation of European colonies in Africa and Asia** Choice (1) is incorrect because the 13 American colonies gained independence in the late 1700s. Choice (3) is incorrect because competition did not lead to cooperation. Choice (4) is incorrect because the Cold War started much later and was not caused by European competition for raw materials.

Lesson 18

Page 117

1. alliance 3. civilians

2. nationalism 4. terrorism

5. **(2) France** The map shows that Estonia and Great Britain were both among the unoccupied Allied countries. So choices (1) and (3) are incorrect. The map shows that

Spain was a neutral nation during World War II, so choice (4) is incorrect.

6. **(4) Great Britain and France declaring war on Germany.** Choice (1) is incorrect because Great Britain and Germany did not become allies. Choice (2) is incorrect because Germany already had a dictator. Choice (3) is incorrect because the Allies declared war on Germany.

7. **(3) two atomic bombs were dropped on the country.** Choice (1) is incorrect because by 1945, many Pacific islands were back in Allied hands. Choice (2) is incorrect because Germany had already surrendered. Choice (4) is incorrect because the Soviet Union did not invade Japan.

GED Skill Strategy, *pages 118–119*

Page 118

Exercise 1:

1. the number of minority soldiers drafted during World War II

2. the number of drafted soldiers

Page 119

Exercise 2:

1. T   2. F   3. T

GED Test-Taking Strategy

Page 121

1. **(2) After 1950, many Nigerians moved to Lagos to find work.** Choice (1) is incorrect because there is no information about the total population of Nigeria in the graph. Choice (3) is incorrect because the paragraph doesn't compare Nigeria with other African nations. Choice (4) is incorrect because there is no information about other Nigerian cities in either the paragraph or the graph.

Unit 4 GED Test Practice, *pages 122–124*

Page 122

1. **(3) The Soviet Union collapsed while they were on *Mir*.** Choices (1) and (4) are incorrect because none of these things would cause people to lose their citizenship in a country. Choice (2) is not true.

2. **(4) They came from different parts of the Soviet Union.** Choice (1) is incorrect because the political views of the astronauts are not discussed. Choices (2) and (3) are incorrect because nothing in the passage supports them.

Page 123

3. **(2) 19%** Choice (1) is the percent of English who could read and write from 1300 to 1500. Choice (3) is the percent of English who could read and write in 1700. Choice (4) is the percent of English who could read and write in 1800.

4. **(1) The literacy of the English population increased from 1300 to 1800.** Choices (2) and (4) are details from the graph. Choice (3) is incorrect because nothing on the graph tells you that literacy is a resource.

5. **(4) Few people needed to read and write for their work.** Choice (1) is incorrect because few people could read and write, indicating these were not important life skills at the time. Choices (2) and (3) are incorrect because if all

children had learned to read, then the literacy rate would not have been only 6 percent at this time.

Page 124

6. **(1) Sparta needed to prevent its slaves from taking over.** Choices (2), (3), and (4) are incorrect because they are not the reason that all citizens were drafted into the army in Sparta.

7. **(4) The army was well-trained and effective**. Choice (1) is incorrect because soldiers were not volunteers. Every citizen had to be a soldier. Choice (2) is incorrect because most residents of Sparta were slaves. Slaves were not in the army. Choice (3) is incorrect because women were not in the army.

Unit 5 Lesson 19

Page 129

1. depression   **2.** inflation   **3.** shortage

4. **(4) shells** According to the timeline on page 126, shells were the first form of money. Choice (2) is incorrect because iron and lead coins were not used as money until 200 years after shells. Choice (3) is incorrect because silver and gold coins were not used as money until 700 years after shells. Choice (1) is incorrect because paper money was not used until 2,000 years after shells.

5. **(2) a period of growth** Choice (1) is incorrect because a depression only occasionally follows a recession. Choices (3) and (4) are incorrect because they are characteristics of a recession, not what follows a recession.

6. Answers will vary. Here is a sample answer: During a boom time, businesses do well and hire workers. The unemployment rate is low. During a recession, businesses may lay off people or stop hiring. The unemployment rate is high.

GED Skill Strategy, *pages 130–131*

Page 130

Exercise 1: (2) Owning stock can be risky. Choice (1) is incorrect because the paragraph indicates that many stock owners lost all their money. Choice (3) is incorrect because only those people who have all of their savings in stocks would lose all their money when the stock market crashed.

Page 131

Exercise 2: Answers will vary. Here are sample answers:

1. Demand grows for products that use new technology. The demand for products using older technology decreases.

2. DVD players became substitutes for VCRs. The demand for DVD players grew, and the demand for VCRs fell.

Lesson 20

Page 135

1. interest   **2.** budget   **3.** income

4. **(2) The budget process is based on estimates.** Choice (1) is incorrect because Congress sets the budget before tax income is known. Choice (3) is incorrect because politics is involved in any government decision, including setting the yearly budget. Choice (4) is incorrect because

the president only proposes the budget. Congress has the power to change it.

5. (1) after the president has asked for a new budget. Choices (2), (3), and (4) are incorrect because the OMB makes its budget before Congress votes and before taxes are collected.

6. (2) after the Federal Reserve interest rate goes up. Choice (1) is incorrect because bank interest rates change in response to the Federal Reserve interest rates. Choice (3) is incorrect because the number of customers a bank has does not necessarily affect the bank's interest rates. Choice (4) is incorrect because banks issue mortgages as part of their business, whether interest rates are rising, falling, or remaining steady.

GED Skill Strategy, *pages 136–137*

Page 136

Exercise 1:

1. Jay and Dina's monthly income   **2.** $1,200

Page 137

Exercise 2:

1. F   **2.** T   **3.** T   **4.** F

GED Test-Taking Strategy

Page 139

1. (1) The time needed to make a car decreased sharply. Choices (2), (3), and (4) are incorrect because the manufacturing time went from more than twelve hours to one and one half hours.

2. (3) 2003 Choices (1), (2), and (4) are incorrect because 2003 is the highest point on the line. That was when unemployment peaked.

Unit 5 GED Test Practice, *pages 140–142*

Page 140

1. (1) The excise tax is lower there. Choice (2) is incorrect because people will not travel in order to pay more taxes. Choice (3) is incorrect because the reason is cost, not brands. Choice (4) is incorrect because the passage indicates that differences in the cost of cigarettes are caused by differences in excise taxes.

2. (4) Raise the excise tax on gasoline and other fuels. Choice (1) is incorrect because charging federal sales tax would affect the sale of all items, not just the sale of fuels. Choices (2) and (3) are incorrect because lowering the excise tax on cars and fuels would probably lead to an increase in car sales and fuel consumption.

Page 141

3. (2) the 2004 budget of the Department of Homeland Security Choice (1) is incorrect because the graph shows only the budget, not the actual expenses. Choice (3) is incorrect because the graph does not show the federal budget, just the budget for one department. Choice (4) is incorrect because the graph shows the budget for the entire department.

4. (4) border and transportation security Choices (1), (2), and (3) are incorrect because less money is budgeted for these items than for border and transportation security.

5. (3) preventing and responding to terrorism in the United States Choice (1) is incorrect because the department spends tax dollars to achieve its goals, not as an end in itself. Choice (2) is incorrect because nothing in the graph shows that the department trains the armed services. Choice (4) is incorrect because all the budget items involve activity in the United States.

Page 142

6. **(2) Workers become bored.** Choices (1), (3), and (4) are incorrect because they would not result from repeating small tasks again and again.

7. **(3) Workers should work on larger segments of the product.** Choice (1) is incorrect because breaking the tasks down into very small parts is what causes worker boredom. Choice (2) is incorrect because slowing the line would only increase boredom. Choice (4) is incorrect because speeding up the line just makes it hard for workers to keep up. It doesn't relieve boredom.

Social Studies Posttest, *pages 143–149*

Page 143

1. **(2) Florida.** The southern tip of Florida is in a tropical climate zone. All other choices have hot summers and mild winters.

Page 144

2. **(2) The people who moved west under the Homestead Act were braver than those who stayed in the East.** This statement is an opinion because there is nothing in the passage about the qualities of those who settled in the West and those who stayed in the East. All other choices are facts stated in the passage.

3. **(3) Both caused people to move west.** Choice (1) is incorrect because the Gold

Rush was not started by the government. Choice (2) is incorrect because the Homestead Act was passed in 1862. Choice (4) is incorrect because the Homestead Act did encourage people to settle down in the West.

Page 145

4. **(3) 1980** Find 40 percent on the vertical axis. Then read across to find the first bar higher than the 40 percent line. That is 1980.

5. **(4) There has been a steady increase in the number of women in the work force.** The height of the bars increases, showing a steady growth in the number of women in the work force over the years.

6. **(3) A higher percentage of children born in 2000 have mothers who work than did children born in 1920.** Choices (1), (2), and (4) are incorrect because the graph does not show how much women are paid or how much education they have.

Page 146

7. **(2) the islands of Sicily, Sardinia, and Corsica** Choice (1) is incorrect because Rome controlled Italy before the Punic Wars. Choice (3) is incorrect because Rome gained Spain after the second Punic War. Choice (4) is incorrect because Rome did not gain control of Carthage after either of the two wars.

8. **(4) Carthage wanted revenge for its loss in the first war.** Choices (1) and (2) are incorrect because Hannibal's march and Rome's invasion of North Africa were part of the second Punic War. They were not causes of the war. Choice (3) is incorrect because it was a result of the second Punic War.

9. **(4) $2,487 million** According to the label on the graph, that is the amount of aid given for food stamps. Choice (1) is the amount given for child nutrition programs. Choice (2) is the amount given for women, infants, and children programs. Choice (3) is the amount given for other programs.

10. **(2) More than twice as much was paid for child nutrition programs.** The graph shows that $9,949 million was paid for child nutrition programs. That is more than twice as much as the $4,206 million paid for programs for women, infants, and children. You can also compare the size of the wedges to get the correct answer.

11. **(2) Most aid helps pay for food and nutrition programs.** Choices (1) and (4) are incorrect because there is no specific state information on the graph. Choice (3) is incorrect because there is no specific information about aid to farmers.

12. **(2) about 2,000,000 people** Find 1980 on the horizontal axis. Then find the point above it on the trend line. Read across to the horizontal axis. There were about 2,000,000 people on active duty that year.

13. **(3) More Americans served in 1970 than in 1950 or 1990.** The armed services had the most people on active duty in 1970. In 1950 and 1990, there were fewer people on active duty. Choice (1) is incorrect because the armed services shrank after 1970. Choice (2) is incorrect because the armed services grew after

1950. Choice (4) is incorrect because the graph does not give information about deaths.

14. **(2) American voters** Choice (1) is incorrect because nothing in the cartoon indicates that the couple is retired. Choice (3) is incorrect because the candidates are on TV, not on the sofa. Choice (4) is incorrect because the cartoon deals with politics, not consumer advertising.

15. **(3) during a debate between presidential candidates** This can be inferred from the newspaper headline. It can also be inferred from the comment about the candidate's answer to a question. Choices (1) and (2) are incorrect because the two people watching television are talking during a political campaign, not during a president's speech. Choice (4) is incorrect because political debates take place before, not after, an election.

16. **(2) Debates have limited value because candidates can avoid answering questions.** The cartoonist shows this by the woman's words. She points out that the candidate did not answer the question. The other choices are all facts related to the cartoon.